JEAN FISCHER

Writing
GRATITUDE
~ ON ~
My Heart

A 6-WEEK BIBLE
MEMORY
DEVOTIONAL

BARBOUR BOOKS
An Imprint of Barbour Publishing, Inc.

Published by Barbour Books, an imprint of Barbour Publishing, Inc., 1810 Barbour Drive, Uhrichsville, Ohio 44683, www.barbourbooks.com

Our mission is to inspire the world with the life-changing message of the Bible.

Member of the
Evangelical Christian
Publishers Association

Printed in China.

Week 1
A GRATEFUL HEART

Thou art my God, and I will praise thee: thou art my God, I will exalt thee.

PSALM 118:28

"Thank God!" Two little words usually said with a sigh of relief and spoken every day all over the world. Maybe you've uttered them yourself when unexpected trouble came your way. "Thank God the storm missed us!" "Thank God my family and I are safe!" "Thank God I'm healthy!" "Thank God I had enough money in my account!" Maybe you've even said the words casually: "TGIF, thank God it's Friday." Words and ideas once thought-provoking can become so routine their original meanings get lost. Little phrases slip into our vocabulary and become clichés and, sadly, "Thank God" is one of them.

Take a minute right now to finish this sentence with the first word that comes to mind: "Thank God I'm _____." Did you say "alive"? It's the most common response. We thank God for life, for that precious moment He brought us into the world. Life is the first of His immeasurable blessings, and we have endless other reasons to thank Him. As our relationship with our heavenly Father grows and we learn to recognize His goodness, the phrase "Thank God" takes on new meaning. It becomes "Praise God!" When your baby takes her first steps, praise God. When that miserable flu you've had for weeks goes away, praise Him. When your spouse expresses his love for you by readily helping with household chores or taking you out for a romantic dinner, sing praises to the Lord! As your eyes open to God's blessings, you will discover that life overflows with reasons to be grateful to Him. Then, like David illustrates in the Bible, praising God becomes a welcome habit. "Seven times a day I praise you," David said (Psalm 119:164 NIV).

How many times a day do you praise God? There are different ways you can communicate your gratitude. In this six-week devotional study, you'll explore some of the reasons to be grateful to God and discover ways of expressing your thanks to Him. *Writing Gratitude on My Heart* will help you enjoy life fully, lift your spirits, and lead you toward a more positive perspective when obstacles get in your way.

You'll begin each week with a single scripture verse you can memorize. The tear-out index cards in this book contain the verses to help you remember so you can write each one on your heart. Your daily devotional explores the weekly verse in depth, illustrating how God's Word and its teaching affect your inner thoughts, salvation, eternity, relationships, and everyday life. Each devotion is followed by "The Blank Page," where you will find ideas for applying what you've learned, and "The Last Word" to give you even more to think about by digging deeper into words, ideas, scripture memorization, and more.

Thou art my God, and I will praise thee:
thou art my God, I will exalt thee.
PSALM 118:28

❧ The Blank Page ❧

Look around you and notice the most ordinary things. Use all your senses to take in the things you can see, hear, taste, smell, or touch—things so mundane that they rarely, if ever, enter your thoughts. It can be the feel of the chair you're sitting in, the sound of the furnace turning on, the smell of your favorite cologne or scented candle. Grab a piece of paper and a pen, and list three to five of those everyday things. Then write at least one reason to thank God for each of them.

The master storyteller, Hans Christian Andersen, wrote in his book *Shorter Tales*, "The whole world is a series of miracles...but we're so used to them that we call them everyday things."[1] Andersen understood there is much we take for granted. How easily a foot fits into a stocking, how effortlessly one foot leads the other when we walk, the places our feet take us...little things, ordinary things, and each worthy of giving praise to God.

Get in the habit of noticing little everyday miracles, and as you notice each one, say, "Thank You, God!" Soon, you'll discover there's really nothing ordinary in the whole world. Everything is a part of God's plan and is praiseworthy. Praise God right now by reciting to Him this week's scripture verse: "Thou art my God, and I will praise thee: thou art my God, I will exalt thee" (Psalm 118:28).

---

[1] Hans Christian Andersen, *Hans Christian Andersen's Shorter Tales*, trans. Jean Hersholt (New York: Heritage Press, 1948), 47.

The Last Word

The idea of memorizing scripture can be daunting, but it doesn't have to be. There are many different ways to commit a Bible verse to memory.

Repeating a verse is the key to writing it on your heart. Start by using the Bible memory cards. Make each week's card an active part of your daily routine. Practice the verse in the morning while you get ready for the day. Take the card along to your workplace. Say the verse to yourself often, especially when negative feelings like frustration or boredom creep in. At bedtime, repeat the verse again and allow it to run through your thoughts as you fall asleep.

Another technique is to analyze how the scripture applies to your daily life. Say the verse then think about what it means to you personally. Each day think of a different way the verse applies to you and your life.

If you enjoy art or crafts, create something using the verse. If music is your thing, turn the scripture into a song.

You can even pray the scripture. Recite it to God and ask Him to open your heart to the scripture's deeper meaning. Luke 24:45 tells us Jesus opened His disciples' minds so they could understand God's Word. He can do that for you too!

Not everyone learns using the same method. Think about how you prefer to learn, and then choose the method best for you.

Week 1: DAY TWO
BEAUTIFUL SPIRIT, BEAUTIFUL HEART

If someone asked you to describe yourself, would you say that you're beautiful? Some women brag about their beauty, but that's not you. You're humble. Even if you are pretty, you might be reluctant to say so because you know that beauty is more than skin deep.

Jesus' disciple Peter explains how God perceives beauty. He says, "Do not let your beauty come from the outside. It should not be the way you comb your hair or the wearing of gold or the wearing of fine clothes. Your beauty should come from the inside. It should come from the heart. . . . Your beauty should be a gentle and quiet spirit. In God's sight this is of great worth and no amount of money can buy it" (1 Peter 3:3–4 NLV).

First Samuel 16:7 says while humans often define beauty by outward appearances, God looks at the heart. The Bible rarely tells us what its characters looked like. We know that Esther was beautiful and John the Baptist had a rugged appearance. But we know little about what Mary the mother of Jesus looked like, or Ruth and Naomi, or Jesus' friends Mary and Martha, or Jesus Himself. The Bible concentrates instead on the hearts of its people—that's what God does, and that's what we should do too.

A beautiful heart is always grateful. It comes from knowing God, loving Him, and working at becoming more like Him. A beautiful heart, even one that's a work in progress, shines its light on the world. It defies physical beauty and draws others nearer to the beauty of God's Spirit and love.

Physical beauty is fleeting. Time strips the natural color from hair and etches wrinkles onto skin. But nothing can tarnish the beauty of a gentle, quiet spirit and a grateful heart filled with love for God. He made you in His image. Think about that. No one knows what God looks like, but the Bible provides plenty of insight into God's Spirit. He wants you to work toward making your heart beautiful like His.

God says you are beautiful! So, instead of looking into the mirror and giving yourself a score for the way you look, examine your heart. What do you see? Thank God for giving you a beautiful heart that radiates His love out into the world, a heart that grows in gratefulness every day.

Psalm 139:14 (NCV) is a praise prayer and another scripture verse to write on your heart. It's one you can recite to God especially on those days when you look in the mirror and see a bad hair day, wrinkles, or pimples: "[Dear God] I praise you because you made me in an amazing and wonderful way. What you have done is wonderful. I know this very well."

Praise God today. Praise Him with a grateful heart for making you just as you are. You are amazing, wonderful—and beautiful too!

Thou art my God, and I will praise thee:
thou art my God, I will exalt thee.
PSALM 118:28

The Blank Page

Adjectives. Without them, we'd have no words to describe the warm, fuzzy feelings we get when we look up at a star-filled sky or at a glamorous, elegant, white water lily extending its petals above a still, sunlit pond. Thank God for beautiful words and the ability to share them!

Today, jot down adjectives that describe your inner beauty. What character traits are you grateful for? Are you adventurous? Polite? Gregarious? Maybe you are considerate, understanding, and sympathetic. Write down all the positive adjectives you can think of that describe your personality, and don't be shy! It's perfectly okay to acknowledge all the good traits God has blessed you with.

Think about what you can do to make your heart even more beautiful. What are some ways you can connect more deeply with God? How can you better understand His Spirit so you can become more like Him? Consider incorporating your words into creating something to remind you God made you and loves you.

Praise God for you! There is no one on earth just like you. God created you as His unique work of art. He loves you, and you are precious in His sight.

The Last Word

When we work at seeing ourselves and others the way God sees us, we discover that God loves us and wants us to be happy. He even sent His Son, Jesus, to save us from sin so we can have a forever home with Him in heaven. Gratefulness grows in our hearts when we understand that God has positive, loving thoughts toward us. When we practice gratefulness, we learn to focus on goodness and blessings rather than sadness and pain. We become more aware of God's mercy and loving-kindness.

Gratefulness requires a positive attitude. In the Sermon on the Mount, Jesus told His followers, "The eye is the light of the body. If your eye is good, your whole body will be full of light. If your eye is bad, your whole body will be dark. If the light in you is dark, how dark it will be!" (Matthew 6:22–23 NLV).

The apostle Paul prayed about this in Ephesians 1:18 (NIV) when he said, "I pray that the eyes of your heart may be enlightened." Pray today and ask God to open the eyes of your heart so you can be enlightened to view life more optimistically. Ask Him to help you see yourself and others in the same loving way that He sees you.

Week 1: DAY THREE
THE ESSENCE OF GRATEFULNESS

What is gratefulness? In the newsletter *HEALTHbeat*, Harvard Medical School defines it as "a thankful appreciation for what an individual receives, whether tangible or intangible." It explains, "With gratitude, people acknowledge the goodness in their lives.... People usually recognize that the source of that goodness lies at least partially outside themselves. As a result, gratitude also helps people connect to something larger than themselves."[2]

In a gratefulness study done by psychologists Dr. Robert A. Emmons of the University of California, Davis, and Dr. Michael E. McCullough of the University of Miami, three study groups participated in a ten-week experiment. Individuals in the first group wrote down what they were grateful for each week. The second group wrote what had been irritating or upsetting. The third group wrote only on events that had affected them in neither a positive nor negative way. Not surprisingly, those in the first group were more optimistic about their lives. They reported that being in the gratitude group had motivated them to offer help and support to others. You might think of it as God's light shining through them and out into the world! Emmons concluded, "Gratitude is essential if we are to truly understand ourselves." In other words, gratitude begins with you.

Gratitude begins with thanking God you are alive and then finding joy in life, but it goes much deeper. True gratitude is finding joy in life even when life is less than joyful. Being grateful all the

---

2 "Giving Thanks Can Make You Happier," *HEALTHbeat*, https://www.health.harvard.edu/healthbeat/giving-thanks-can-make-you-happier.

time is something you practice and learn. There are days when you will ask yourself, "How can I be grateful when my life is a mess?" On those days, you can build an even stronger connection with God by relying on Him for strength, comfort, and hope. When life gets messy, you find the deepest meaning of gratitude when you pare it down to its very core—gratefulness for God and His love toward you.

God's love is the essence of gratefulness. When you become truly grateful for Him and His loving-kindness, you become more aware of how God extends His love to you and through you into the world. Like those in Emmons and McCullough's gratitude group, you'll be more likely to offer help and support to others when they need it. When you develop a grateful heart, your gratitude becomes contagious.

Have you gone through a rough time in your life that left you with greater empathy for those going through something similar? Because of what you went through, were you able to provide comfort and support to someone else? If you answered yes, then you've experienced God's love. He brought you through that difficult time and gave you a greater capacity to love others—two excellent reasons to be grateful.

How consistent is your gratefulness? Being grateful every day in all circumstances leads to greater happiness and even more reasons to praise God.

Thou art my God, and I will praise thee:
thou art my God, I will exalt thee.
PSALM 118:28

The Blank Page

Memorizing Bible verses about gratefulness, like those in this book, provides you with ready words of praise for the Lord. You can also find examples in the Bible of people who praised God even in the worst of circumstances. Hannah, for example, was devastated by her inability to have children. She was even ridiculed for it. Still, she held on to God, believing in and trusting Him. We can only imagine her gratitude when she gave birth to her son, Samuel. You can read Hannah's prayer of thanksgiving in 1 Samuel 2:1–10. The entire book of Psalms is a study in gratitude as King David pours out his heart and praises to God. The Gospels, the stories of Jesus' life on earth, hold many examples of gratitude when the blind see, the lame walk, and demons leave troubled souls. These are reminders of one more reason to be grateful: God is able in all circumstances to bring good into bad situations.

This week's memory verse says, "Thou art my God, and I will praise thee: thou art my God, I will exalt thee." You can praise God through prayer, by lifting your hands toward Him in worship, and by singing or playing songs of praise.

Your task today is to have a family meeting to discuss ways that you, as a family, can express thankfulness to God. See if you can come up with some unique ways to praise Him. Then make praising God part of your family's daily routine.

The Last Word

Try organizing topics for praise into seven main categories, one for each day of the week:

Monday: Praise God for being your one and only God. Consider His presence and power in your life and how your life is enriched through your personal relationship with Him.

Tuesday: Praise God for material blessings great and small.

Wednesday: Thank Him for the people in your life, not only those whom you love but also those who may have given you trouble and taught you something about life and living.

Thursday: Offer praises to God for the trials you have faced. Think about what you have learned from past difficulties and what you know about how God will lead you through whatever problems you face in the future.

Friday: Praise God for blessing you with skills and talents. What are you good at? Have you blessed others by sharing your gifts?

Saturday: Give praises to Him for the wonders of His creation. Meditate and give thanks for all things amazing and beautiful on earth and in the sky.

Sunday: Praise Him for His Word, the Bible, and what it teaches you.

Week 1: DAY FOUR
ALWAYS THANKFUL

If you spend time surfing the internet, you've seen videos going viral. Something funny catches someone's attention, they record it with their cell phone and decide it's worthy of posting. The video catches on, and it's shared again...and again...baby goats prancing in pajamas, pets behaving badly, adults caught in hilarious situations. Did you see the one about babies tasting lemons for the first time? Oh, those poor little puckered lips! The frowns and heads shaking from side to side. "Oh no. Uh-uh. I don't like this thing." That first taste of lemon can be sour and nasty. It could make you hate lemons for the rest of your life. Or, you could choose to be more optimistic and embrace that well-known expression "When life gives you lemons, make lemonade." There is goodness to be found in almost everything if you choose to look for it.

The classic 1913 novel *Pollyanna* tells the story of a little girl who finds happiness looking for the good in things. Learning gratefulness began with a game Pollyanna played with her father. When a mission box arrived containing crutches instead of the doll she wanted, the goal of the game was to find a reason to be glad. Pollyanna decided she was glad she didn't need those crutches. Continuing to play the game, she was glad she didn't have a mirror because it meant she didn't have to look at the freckles on her face. She was glad she didn't have a picture book because it made her appreciate the view from her window. Pollyanna learned to continually view life with gladness and gratefulness. "When you're hunting for the glad things," she said, "you sort of forget the other kind." Pollyanna's story was wildly popular in its time and was even made into a Disney movie, but ironically, her positive attitude came to be viewed in a negative way. Some people thought she was just too grateful and glad. Today, dictionaries define the word *Pollyanna* as a blindly optimistic person with an overly optimistic attitude. To be a Pollyanna is generally considered not a good thing.

The apostle Paul was a Pollyanna. He lived a life of suffering and gratitude. This once well-to-do Pharisee who had hated and persecuted Christians learned to love and serve God all the time. Even when he was beaten and imprisoned, Paul lived a life overflowing with gratefulness. While in prison, he wrote to his friends, "Be thankful in all circumstances, for this is God's will for you who belong to Christ Jesus" (1 Thessalonians 5:18 NLT).

God wants you to be like Pollyanna and Paul, finding goodness in life even when it gives you lemons. Pollyanna taught her glad game to the worst curmudgeons in her town and won them over. She led others into lives filled with gratefulness to God. Be like Pollyanna. It's a good thing! God's will for you and for everyone is to be forever thankful.

Thou art my God, and I will praise thee:
thou art my God, I will exalt thee.
PSALM 118:28

The Blank Page

In a sermon about praise, Charles Spurgeon said, "It would create an almost miraculous change in some people's lives if they made a point of speaking most of the precious things and least of the worries and ills! Why always the poverty? Why always the pains? Why always the dying child? Why always the husband's small wages? Why always the unkindness of a friend? Why not sometimes—yes, why not *always*—the mercies of the Lord? That is praise and it is to be our everyday garment!"

Today, start playing the glad game by finding something positive when you face a negative. You don't need to be exactly like Pollyanna, speaking on gladness wherever you go, but do your best to find the good in things and be grateful.

Spurgeon also said, "You cannot always be speaking His praise, but you can always be living His praise." So, today begin the good habit of recognizing God's goodness and mercies. See if, as Spurgeon suggested, it creates an almost miraculous change in your life.

In Romans 8:28 (NLV), Paul says, "We know that God makes all things work together for the good of those who love Him and are chosen to be a part of His plan." Look for the good in everything! It's there in plain view waiting to be discovered.

❧ The Last Word ❧

When you work at memorizing a scripture verse, try connecting it with an image, story, or quotation. For example, you could connect this week's memory verse, Psalm 118:28, with an image of Pollyanna finding something new to be glad about and praising God for His goodness: "Thou art my God, and I will praise thee: thou art my God, I will exalt thee"!

You could think about Spurgeon's quotes and turn them into prayers praising God:

"It would create an almost miraculous change in some people's lives if they made a point of speaking most of the precious things and least of the worries and ills!"

"Dear God, I want to make a positive change in my life by praising You for precious things instead of speaking about what worries me. 'Thou art my God, and I will praise thee: thou art my God, I will exalt thee'!"

"You cannot always be speaking His praise, but you can always be living His praise."

"Dear God, I want to live a life of constant praise. 'Thou art my God, and I will praise thee: thou art my God, I will exalt thee'!"

Allow the combination of scripture, stories, images, and quotations to help you write God's Word on your heart.

Week 1: DAY FiVE
THE POWER OF PRAISE

Praise is powerful. When we receive praise, it makes us feel good about ourselves, inspires us to do our best, refreshes and renews us. Praise connects us with others in the most positive way. It acknowledges our best qualities and conveys acceptance and sometimes gratitude and love. C. S. Lewis said, "Praise almost seems to be inner health made audible." Receiving praise is like a balm for hurting and discouraged hearts. It makes us want to become better. It increases our inner strength and power. Receiving praise is wonderful! Still, it's important to note that the power that comes with receiving praise is fleeting. There is another kind of praise that gives us everlasting power. It's the kind of power that comes not by receiving praise but rather by giving it. It's the power that comes from praising God.

When we praise God, we not only express gratitude to Him; we invite Him into our hearts. Praise humbles us as we recognize and affirm God's greatness and His power working within us. It opens us up to receive His blessings. Praise pushes away the darkness that surrounds us and bathes us in God's light. When we embrace God and make Him the center of our attention and praise, we have power over Satan and all the ways he tries to destroy us. With God pouring His power into our hearts, our inner selves feel better. The worries, fears, and anxieties lessen when we accept that God is in control and He loves us. When we offer to God our grateful praise, like C. S. Lewis said, our inner health is made audible. Praise is music to God's ears, and in His presence when we praise Him, our hearts become full of joy (Psalm 16:11).

In this week's memory verse, David says, "Thou art my God, and I will praise thee: thou art my God, I will exalt thee." David praises God for no other reason than the best and most perfect reason: because God is God. David acknowledges God as *his* God, worthy of praise and exaltation. This God, David's God, is your God too. He is worthy of your praise because He is good, merciful, forgiving, never changing, always present—and He wants to be with you now and forever. God wants to pour His awesomeness, His power, into you so you can be the best you can be. He wants you to feel good inside and happy! God wants to pour His power into you so you can share it with others and even help change the world.

Think about how praising God can make you more powerful. Maybe there are areas in your life where your inner health is lacking. Maybe you feel less than confident. Ask God to add His power to those places, to heal what hurts, and to strengthen what's weak. Then, as you see Him working inside you, acknowledge Him with grateful praise.

Thou art my God, and I will praise thee:
thou art my God, I will exalt thee.
Psalm 118:28

The Blank Page

Praise God from whom all Blessings flow,
Praise him all Creatures here below,
Praise him above, ye Heavenly Host.
Praise Father, Son, and Holy Ghost.

This traditional doxology, or praise song, was written in 1674 in England by the Anglican bishop and hymnist Thomas Ken. For many years it was the most common hymn of praise sung at every Protestant Sunday worship service.

In contemporary services, we sing many different songs of praise. Chris Tomlin's "How Great Is Our God," Hillsong's "What a Beautiful Name," and Pat Barrett's "Build My Life" are just a few of the praise songs most often sung in church.

Today as you think about the power of praise, sing your praises to God. First Chronicles 16:9 (NLV) tells us, "Sing to Him. Sing praises to Him. Tell of all His great works." In the car, at home, while making dinner or getting your kids ready for bed, or during your special time of prayer, sing to the Lord. Sing the praise songs you know and love, but also create your own songs of praise. Express your gratefulness to God not only for the countless things He does for you but also because of who He is—your God, the One most worthy of your grateful praise.

The Last Word

Do you wonder what the difference is between a hymn and a praise song? The farmer in this humorous story tries to explain:

> An old farmer went to the city one weekend and attended a big city church. When he came home, his wife asked him how it was. "Well," said the farmer, "it was good. They did something different, though. They sang praise songs instead of hymns."
>
> "Praise songs," said his wife. "What are those?"
>
> "Oh, they're okay. They're sort of like hymns, only different," said the farmer.
>
> "Well, what's the difference?" asked his wife.
>
> The farmer said, "Well it's like this. If I were to say to you: 'Oh Martha, the cows are in the corn,' well, that would be a hymn. If, on the other hand, I were to say to you, 'Oh Martha, Martha, Martha. Oh, Martha, MARTHA, MARTHA, the cows, the big cows, the brown cows, the black cows, the white cows, the black and white cows, the COWS, COWS, COWS, are in the corn, are in the corn, are in the corn, are in the corn, the CORN, CORN, CORN,' well, that would be a praise song!"

Week 1: DAY SiX
SiNG iN EXALTATiON!

When you hear the word *exaltation,* maybe you think of the Christmas song "O Come All Ye Faithful": *Sing choirs of angels, sing in exaltation. Exalt* is a worship word. In this week's memory verse, David says, "Thou art my God, I will exalt thee." Exaltation is a happy, energetic form of grateful praise.

Moses was caring for a flock of sheep when God spoke to him, "Moses, Moses!"

"Here I am," Moses said.

"I am the God of your father, the God of Abraham, the God of Isaac, and the God of Jacob. . . . I have seen the suffering of My people in Egypt. I have heard their cry because of the men who make them work. . . . So I have come down to save them from the power of the Egyptians. I will bring them out of that land to a good big land, to a land flowing with milk and honey. . . . The cry of the people of Israel has come to Me. I have seen what power the Egyptians use to make it hard for them. Now come, and I will send you to Pharaoh so that you may bring My people. . .out of Egypt" (Exodus 3:6–10 NLV).

Moses knew how powerful Pharaoh was. He didn't need God to tell him. He argued with God. "Who am I to go to Pharaoh and bring the people of Israel out of Egypt?" (v. 11). "What if they will not believe me or listen to me?" (Exodus 4:1 NLV). "Lord, I am not a man of words. I have never been. . . . For I am slow in talking and it is difficult for me to speak" (4:10).

God replied, "Who has made man's mouth? Who makes a man

not able to speak or hear? Who makes one blind or able to see? Is it not I, the Lord? So go now. And I will be with your mouth. I will teach you what to say" (Exodus 4:11–12 NLV).

"I will be with you. And this will be something special for you to see to know that I have sent you: When you have brought the people out of Egypt, you will worship [Me] at this mountain" (Exodus 3:12 NLV).

Moses did what God said, and with God's mighty power strengthening him, Moses led the Israelites out of Egypt. In Exodus 15:1–2 (NLV), we see him leading the people in a happy song of exaltation: "I will sing to the Lord, for He is praised for His greatness. . . . The Lord is my strength and song. He is the One Who saves me. He is my God and I will praise Him. He is my father's God and I will honor Him."

Maybe, like Moses, you feel God leading you where you'd rather not go. Trust Him. He might have something special in mind for you just as He did for Moses, something worthy of exaltation.

Thou art my God, and I will praise thee:
thou art my God, I will exalt thee.
PSALM 118:28

❧ The Blank Page ❧

"Praise the Lord! For it is good to sing praises to our God. For it is pleasing and praise is right." These are David's first words in Psalm 147 (NLV). He continues his psalm listing reasons to praise God:

- *He heals those who have a broken heart.*
- *He heals their sorrows.*
- *He knows the number of the stars;*
  He gives names to all of them.
- *His understanding has no end.*
- *He gives rain for the earth.*
- *He makes grass grow on the mountains.*
- *He gives food to the animals.*

Read the entire psalm in your Bible.

Your task today is to create a praise box that you can use throughout the year. It doesn't have to be anything fancy, just something to hold pieces of paper—your own praise statements to God. At the end of each day, write this sentence on a piece of paper and fill in the blank:

Dear God, today I praise You for _____.

There are many different reasons to praise God. Think about what you are grateful for: friends and family, things in nature, accomplishments, provisions, God's faithfulness, your salvation.... On days when you feel grumpy or sad or you find it hard to be grateful, pour out your praise statements and read them.

The Last Word

In Hebrew, the word *exalt* means to lift up. When we sing praise songs and lift our hands up toward God, it is a symbol of surrendering to Him, a sign of our gratefulness and of inviting Him to come down and empower us with His Holy Spirit. The lifting of hands is nothing new. In the Old Testament, David says, "May the lifting up of my hands be like the evening gift given on the altar in worship" (Psalm 141:2 NLV).

In Nehemiah 8, Ezra, a religious leader of the Jews, reminds the people of the laws God sent down to them through Moses. He opens the book of the Law, and for hours he reads it to them. "Then Ezra gave honor and thanks to the Lord the great God. And all the people answered, 'Let it be so!' while lifting up their hands. [Then] they bowed low with their faces to the ground and worshiped the Lord" (Nehemiah 8:6 NLV). Bowing before God, kneeling, is another way of exalting Him, of lifting Him up. When we kneel in prayer, we acknowledge His superiority and greatness. When we kneel, we humble ourselves before God in gratefulness and yield to His mighty power.

Week 1: DAY SEVEN
PUTTING IT ALL TOGETHER

Thinking about this past week, ask yourself these five questions:

1. *Have I grown in gratefulness?*
2. *Have I found more reasons to thank God?*
3. *Do I have a more optimistic attitude?*
4. *Am I able to be grateful even on bad days?*
5. *Do I praise God more often?*

Studies show the benefits to having a grateful heart. Gratitude helps us to be more satisfied with life. It improves mental health and can even help us cope with physical illness. Grateful people report sleeping better, and they often have higher self-esteem. Practicing gratefulness can lead to a deeper connection with others through empathy, sympathy, and sensitivity. When we act toward others with an attitude of gratitude, we open the door to new and more positive relationships.

We aren't born grateful. True gratefulness develops slowly. It grows as our relationship with God deepens and matures. True gratefulness is much more than being thankful for God's blessings. It is being grateful because God *is*. In the Bible, God repeatedly says, "I Am." His existence is the root of all things good, and from that root gratefulness emerges, grows, and thrives. We find infinite reasons to praise God because He is our creator, provider, healer, friend, counselor, teacher, safe place, tower of strength. When we invite Him into our hearts, God is with us wherever we go, no matter what, forever. We are grateful because He promises never to leave or reject us. If we stay focused on Him and keep our eyes open, we can be sure that He will give us many reasons to be grateful in every circumstance all the days of our lives.

In the Bible, Hannah prays, "My heart is happy in the Lord" (1 Samuel 2:1 NLV). When we exalt God with praise, it leads to a kind of happiness that is centered on Him instead of things and experiences. We develop a heart that is happier because our eyes are always open to God's blessings. We can find something positive in almost everything. In those times when we can't see God through the ugliness, sadness, or anger, we can still have a grateful heart, knowing that He *is*.

He is there.

He sees.

He knows.

He has a plan.

And in His own time, He will make all things perfectly good and new.

Work at building a grateful heart. If you concentrate on being grateful, it will affect not only your life; it will affect the lives of those around you as well. Gratefulness will make you easier to be with and also make it easier for you to get along with difficult people. Be grateful because you are here. You are alive and part of God's world. Be grateful for your successes, your failures, and your faith. Then as your gratefulness grows, you will discover yourself becoming tougher, wiser, and stronger.

Thou art my God, and I will praise thee:
thou art my God, I will exalt thee.
PSALM 118:28

The Blank Page

Have you memorized this week's Bible verse? If not, do it now: "Thou art my God, and I will praise thee: thou art my God, I will exalt thee" (Psalm 118:28).

Memorizing scripture is important because it provides you with a deeper understanding of God. As you study the Bible, it helps you view the world through God's eyes. His words lead you to be brave; they comfort, motivate, challenge, heal, provide peace and stability, and give you an overabundance of reasons to be grateful.

If you believe memorizing scripture is too hard or unnecessary, do it anyway. Don't allow anything to get in your way. Write God's words on your heart so they will be with you wherever you go.

Share the verses you've memorized. Deuteronomy 6:6–7 (CEV) says, "Memorize his laws and tell them to your children over and over again. Talk about them all the time, whether you're at home or walking along the road or going to bed at night, or getting up in the morning."

Use the index cards in this book to help you. Write the words until you have them memorized. Use the other memory tips you've learned this week or your own. There is no wrong way to go about it.

The author of Psalm 119:105 (NKJV) wrote: "[God] Your word is a lamp to my feet and a light to my path." Keep God's words in your heart, and allow them to light your way.

The Last Word

Dear God, please guide me toward a more grateful heart. Make my gratefulness grow. Open my eyes to Your blessings, and I will humble myself before You. I will lift my hands toward You in thankfulness and praise. Give me a grateful heart not only in good times but also during times that challenge me or cause sadness or pain. Give me a heart that is always happy in the Lord.

How great is my God and worthy of praise! How great You are for being, for creating me and giving me life. Thank You, dear God, for giving me so many reasons to be grateful. Amen.

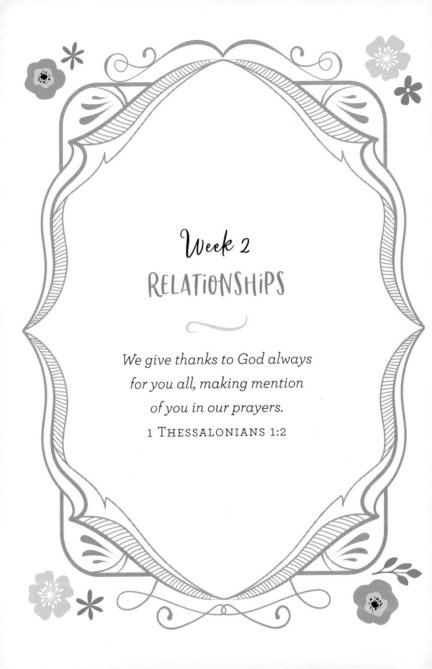

Week 2

RELATIONSHIPS

*We give thanks to God always
for you all, making mention
of you in our prayers.*

1 THESSALONIANS 1:2

Week 2: DAY ONE
LOVE ONE ANOTHER

Paul's letter to his friends, the leaders of the church in Corinth, begins: "I always thank my God for you because of the grace God has given you in Christ Jesus" (1 Corinthians 1:4 NCV).

The goal of Paul's letter was to set things straight in a divided and troubled church. But instead of starting with criticism, Paul thanked God for blessing his friends with grace—God's favor and kindness toward them. In other words, Paul thanked God for the goodness He bestowed on Paul's friends. The church in Corinth was a young church where people were not getting along or respecting their leaders. The people behaved badly by participating in activities Paul knew weren't right with God. Still, Paul saw God's goodness there, and he thanked God for it on the Corinthians' behalf. God loved these people even if they were behaving badly, and so did Paul.

Paul sets for us another example of gratefulness. We can be grateful that when we see others out of sync with God's will, God is in that situation and working to make it right. Paul didn't overlook his friends' behavior, but he was able to look beyond it and thank God for showing them grace. Because Paul loved his friends, he also interceded by praying for their redemption. The great evangelist Oswald Chambers said, "True intercession involves bringing the person, or the circumstance that seems to be crashing in on you, before God, until you are changed by His attitude toward that person or circumstance. . . . Intercession is putting yourself in God's place; it is having His mind and His perspective."[3] That's what Paul did, and that should be our goal too.

It's easy to be grateful for the people in our lives when they please us. But when disagreements happen, our gratefulness can diminish. In those times, we need to do what Paul did and try to see others through God's eyes.

Jesus gave this command: "Love each other. You must love each other as I have loved you" (John 13:34 NCV). It's not always easy obeying that command. But Paul shows us we can find something to be grateful for even when others are disobedient or make trouble. By trying to see them through God's eyes, we can pray for them, love them, and thank God that He has power to turn any situation around. We can also see how our relationships help shape us and bring us closer to our heavenly Father.

Think about those people in your life who you are most thankful for. The ones you are closest to get the lion's share of your gratefulness. But what about those near the bottom of your gratefulness list or those not even on it? God loves them too, and even if you can find little else to be grateful for in those relationships, you can thank God for His presence and for what He is doing in their lives.

We give thanks to God always for you all,
making mention of you in our prayers.
1 THESSALONIANS 1:2

---

3   Oswald Chambers, "Intercessory Prayer," *My Utmost for His Highest*, retrieved January 15, 2020, https://utmost.org/intercessory-prayer.

❧ The Blank Page ❧

This week is about relationships. Today, think about people who lead you toward negative feelings, whose personalities, ideas, or values are so different from yours that you have trouble loving or even liking them.

Write down some ways you can pray for those people with gratefulness in your heart. Like Paul, you can thank God for being with them and for showing them grace. You can also thank God for loving them, wanting them to live according to His will, meeting their daily needs, and for His power in their lives. You might also want to thank God for helping you to see others through His eyes, helping you to be patient and kind toward them, helping you to love them, and helping you to learn more about yourself through your relationships with them. Search your heart for more reasons to be grateful for those who might not otherwise make it onto your gratefulness list.

When you pray for others with a grateful heart, you obey Jesus' command to love one another. As you work toward praying for others as Jesus might pray for them, your relationship with Jesus becomes even stronger, and you'll begin to notice a change in your negative feelings toward others.

❧ The Last Word ❧

Here's a fun way to memorize this week's Bible verse: "We give thanks to God always for you all, making mention of you in our prayers" (1 Thessalonians 1:2). Make a collage using the scripture verse and pictures of people you thank God for. An internet search will lead you to free collage makers where you can create a digital collage online, or you might want to make a paper collage using a mix of photographs or a variety of materials (photos, newspaper and magazine clippings, embellishments). You could even create a three-dimensional collage inside a shadow box or other object using the Bible verse, photographs, and items that remind you of the people in your collage. Consider making your work of art frameable, something you will display, see often, and associate with the scripture verse.

Scripture collages make great handmade gifts for special occasions and holidays. If you enjoy this activity, make personalized collages for the people you love. Think of a Bible verse you associate with each person or one you know will be an inspiration. When you give your scripture collages, include gift tags inscribed with the scripture verses. You could share with receivers that you've been memorizing scripture and invite them to commit their verse to memory too.

Week 2: DAY TWO
ALL THE WORLD'S CHILDREN

Kids. Precious gifts from God who teach us unconditional love, patience, tenderness, and humility. They make us laugh. Sometimes they test our strength. They give us a greater purpose in life by challenging us to be better adults. Just when we think we have things figured out, our kids teach us something new. They lead us to savor the little everyday moments, to be surprised, and to accept possibility. There are countless reasons to be grateful for our kids, but the greatest is that they're ours.

The Bible says children are our inheritance from God. He gives them to us with the humbling responsibility of raising them to carry out His work here on earth. As a parent, you focus on your own children, but you also have an obligation to all the children in the world.

In 2019, 26 percent of the world's population was under fifteen years of age.[4] Think about that. Adults in the world today have an opportunity to inspire a quarter of the globe's population to build a better future. In 1996, while giving a speech to schoolchildren in Long Beach, California, President Bill Clinton quoted Abraham Lincoln saying, "A child is a person who is going to carry on what you have started. He is going to sit where you are sitting, and when you are gone, attend to those things you think are important. You may adopt all of the policies you please, but how they are carried out depends on him. He will assume control of your cities, states,

---

4   Erin Duffin, "World Population by Age and Region 2019," retrieved January 18, 2020, https://www.statista.com/statistics/265759/world-population-by-age-and-region/.

and nations. He is going to move in and take over your churches, schools, universities, and corporations. The fate of humanity is in his hands."[5] That sets into perspective what an awesome responsibility we have when raising our children.

Proverbs 22:6 (NLV) says, "Bring up a child by teaching him the way he should go, and when he is old he will not turn away from it." You will teach your own children the way they should go, but you can also help lead the children in your community and beyond toward building a better future. You can volunteer in your church, schools, and at community events. You can become a mentor. You can encourage children around the world by contributing to charitable organizations, supporting Christian missionaries, or sponsoring a child in a developing country. You can teach your kids to be aware of the challenges and have respect for children living in other parts of the world and to connect with kids from varying ethnicities and cultures. Above all, you can be a role model for every child you come in contact with.

God thinks so highly of you that He's put you in charge of all the world's children. He gives you the responsibility of helping them establish principles that will shape their values, beliefs, and behaviors and lead them to what matters most—loving Him and loving others. What a blessing and reason to be grateful!

We give thanks to God always for you all,
making mention of you in our prayers.
1 THESSALONIANS 1:2

---

5   "Clinton Focuses Nation on School Uniforms," Long Beach Unified School District, http://www.lbusd.k12.ca.us/Departments/Uniforms/article_13.cfm.

The Blank Page

"My Heart Leaps Up"

BY WILLIAM WORDSWORTH

My heart leaps up when I behold a rainbow in the sky:
So was it when my life began;
So is it now I am a man;
So be it when I shall grow old, or let me die!
The Child is father of the Man;
And I could wish my days to be
Bound each to each by natural piety.[6]

The words of Wordsworth's poem remind us to hold on to the joys of childhood. Today, think about the special memories you have from when you were a kid.

* *What things in nature, like the rainbow in Wordsworth's poem, made you pause and wonder?*

* *Who were your friends and what did you enjoying doing together?*

* *Where did you like to go?*

* *What gave you the greatest joy?*

* *When did you feel most loved?*

* *Which people led you into the future and helped you become the person you are today?*

As you recall each memory, give thanks to God.

Never lose sight of childhood joy and the simple, often unnoticed things. Look at the world through the eyes of a child sometimes and see if it alters your perspective.

---

6   William Wordsworth, *The Complete Poetical Works* (London: Macmillan and Co., 1888); Bartleby.com, 1999, www.bartleby.com/145/.

❧ The Last Word ❧

Billy Graham said, "The greatest legacy one can pass on to one's children and grandchildren is not money or other material things accumulated in one's life, but rather a legacy of character and faith." His is one of many great quotes that will inspire you as a person responsible for leading the next generation into adulthood. Here are five more:

"Each day of our lives we make deposits in the memory banks of our children." [7] *—Charles R. Swindoll*

"Children are the living messages we send to a time we will not see." [8] *—Neil Postman*

"Every child you encounter is a divine appointment." [9] *—Wess Stafford*

"Children are like wet cement; whatever falls on them makes an impression." [10] *—Haim Ginott*

"If I could relive my life, I would devote my entire ministry to reaching children for God!" [11] *—Dwight L. Moody*

7   Chuck Swindoll, *The Strong Family: Growing Wise in Family Life* (New York: Multnomah Press, 1991), 38

8   Neil Postman, *The Disappearance of Childhood* (New York: Knopf Doubleday Publishing Group, 2011), x

9   Wess Stafford, *Too Small to Ignore: Why the Least of These Matters Most* (Colorado Springs, CO: WaterBrook, 2007), 9.

10   Reader's Digest, ed., *Quotable Quotes* (New York: The Reader's Digest Association, 1997), 58.

11   Kenneth W. Osbeck, *Amazing Grace: 366 Inspiring Hymn Stories for Daily Devotions*, 2nd ed. (Grand Rapids, MI: Kregel Publications, 2010), 70.

Week 2: DAY THREE
THE GRATEFUL SPOUSE

"Marrying a man is like buying something you've been admiring for a long time in a shop window. You may love it when you get it home, but it doesn't always go with everything else in the house!"[12] This humorous quote comes from author and playwright Jean Kerr. It's true; marriage isn't always easy. It takes a lot of compromise, patience, and forgiveness to make a marriage work. As Kerr's quote suggests, sometimes a marriage needs remodeling. You look at it and begin to see little things that should be fixed. Over time, those little things can morph into bigger things until remodeling no longer seems like an option and you decide you're ready for something new. But, before you allow that to happen, take time to adjust your focus.

Thinking too much about what needs fixing makes it difficult to be grateful for what you have. Maybe you and your spouse have been arguing about the house you live in. There's not enough space; it's too far from work; you want to move, he doesn't. But right now, in the moment, you both can be thankful for having a roof over your heads, a safe place to relax at the end of the day, a place called home. Setting aside the argument, you still love each other, and that's the core reason to be grateful.

We think marriage should be a fifty-fifty partnership. But in truth, marriage is a balancing act. The goal is keeping the scale teetering near the middle and not allowing it to tip too far either way for too long. It's a tricky thing to accomplish and something

---

12   Jean Kerr, *The Snake Has All the Lines* (New York: Doubleday & Co., 1960), 121.

that has to be practiced every day. It requires keeping your eyes on the scale and making it a priority. When it dips, then one partner has to do something quickly to balance it out.

One way is to make gratefulness a routine part of your marriage. When things get tense, agree to stop and focus on what in your relationship you're grateful for. Even when things aren't tense, end each day telling your spouse at least one thing in your marriage you are thankful for. You might be surprised by the positive effect this one little change can have on your relationship.

When the scale drops too far one way or the other, there's still hope of bringing it back near the middle by focusing on the big picture instead of the big problem. The big picture is God. Keeping Him as your focal point, trusting Him, and having faith in His power will guide you through the rough spots in your marriage. On those days when you feel your partner has let you down, you can be grateful that God never will.

Does your marriage need remodeling? Shift your focus from what's wrong to what's right. Let that be the starting point. Try viewing your marriage through a new lens. Gratefulness can't fix everything, but it might help you to weather the storms together.

We give thanks to God always for you all,
making mention of you in our prayers.
1 Thessalonians 1:2

❧ The Blank Page ❧

Find some quiet time today, and make a list of reasons you are grateful for your spouse. Write down as many as you can think of. Then, every day, choose one of the reasons on your list, and find a way to express gratitude to your partner. You could leave a note on the bedside table or on the bathroom mirror, send a text, plan a date night to celebrate your gratefulness. . .the list goes on and on.

When you create your list, go beyond the reasons for your thankfulness and cite specific examples.

* *I'm grateful for my husband because he makes me laugh.*
* *His jokes are terrible, but the way he tells them is always funny.*
* *He does silly stuff, and he doesn't care who's watching.*
* *He can laugh at himself when he does something clumsy.*

When you dig deep for examples, your gratefulness will grow.

Expressing gratitude in your marriage can help you connect with a deeper level of intimacy. Notice the little things your partner does that make you happy. Remember to say thank you. Use words and examples to express your love. Say, "I love you because. . ." and say it often.

❦ The Last Word ❦

Ask God to reveal to you those little everyday things your spouse does that you might not think of.

- ❋ *He's always on time.*
- ❋ *He enjoys playing with the kids.*
- ❋ *He picks up his dirty clothes.*
- ❋ *He turns off his cell phone when we're eating dinner.*
- ❋ *He puts gas in the cars and changes the oil.*
- ❋ *He's good at fixing things.*
- ❋ *He pays the bills.*
- ❋ *He helps put the kids to bed.*
- ❋ *He takes messages and tells me when someone calls.*
- ❋ *He gets along with my parents.*
- ❋ *He knows what to do when the computer crashes.*
- ❋ *He gives the dog a bath.*
- ❋ *He doesn't mind changing diapers.*
- ❋ *He helps with the laundry.*

In an interview with Oprah Winfrey, author Eckhart Tolle said, "The present moment is your life. It's nowhere else—never, ever. So, no matter what the situation is, when you align yourself with the present moment, find something to be grateful for."[13] Get into the habit of gratefulness in the moment. Throughout the day, observe all the mundane things your spouse does that are so ordinary and expected they slip by unnoticed. Be aware of them! Be grateful for them, and express your gratitude.

---

13 "Oprah Talks to Eckhart Tolle," Oprah.com, http://www.oprah.com/spirit/oprah-talks-to-eckhart-tolle/5.

Week 2: DAY FOUR
TRUE FRIENDSHIP

Loyalty, *commitment*, and *self-sacrifice*—these three words describe David and Jonathan's friendship in the Bible. David was a rising star in King Saul's court, but David's popularity caused Saul to become jealous and turn against him. The king plotted to have David killed, and had it not been for Jonathan, the king's plan would have succeeded. What's key to the story is that Jonathan was the king's son. The Bible says, "David and Jonathan became best friends. Jonathan thought as much of David as he did of himself" (1 Samuel 18:1 CEV). Jonathan had to choose between loyalty to his father—the king—or his friend David, and he chose David. Jonathan's choice was based on more than their friendship. It was a choice of good over evil. Jealousy was at the root of King Saul's anger. David had done nothing wrong. He was still worthy of Jonathan's loyalty, so Jonathan remained committed to their friendship. He was willing to sacrifice his own safety, his relationship with his father, and even never seeing David again to make sure David stayed safe and alive. That's a true friend.

Ruth and Naomi's Bible story is similar, only theirs was a friendship formed inside a family. Ruth was Naomi's daughter-in-law. When both Ruth and Naomi lost their husbands, Ruth could have chosen to leave Naomi and make a new life without her. Instead, she promised never to leave Naomi. Even when Naomi unselfishly told Ruth to go and be happy, Ruth said, "Please don't tell me to leave you. . . . I will go where you go, I will live where you live; your people will be my people, your God will be my God.

I will die where you die and be buried beside you. May the LORD punish me if we are ever separated, even by death!" (Ruth 1:16–17 CEV). What a beautiful example of a loyal, loving friend.

These two stories illustrate the words of Proverbs 17:17 (CEV): "A friend is always a friend, and relatives are born to share our troubles." They help us to understand God's idea of true friendship: loyalty, commitment, and self-sacrifice. Do you have a friend who exhibits those qualities? If so, you have an extraordinary reason to be thankful.

True friends can make your gratefulness meter shoot up to 100 percent. Like Jonathan, a true friend stands by her commitment to you even when others turn against you. A true friend is like Naomi; she takes you with her into the future and refuses to leave you behind. She is always a friend, sharing with you the good times and also sharing your troubles.

Do any of your friendships stand out like David and Jonathan's or Ruth and Naomi's? Which friendships could you never see your life without? These are your best friends, your true friends. Thank God for them, make them a priority, and remember to show them that you're grateful.

We give thanks to God always for you all,
making mention of you in our prayers.
1 THESSALONIANS 1:2

The Blank Page

"You can count on me." Have you said that to a close friend? Maybe she's said it to you. Whether you need someone to pick up your kids after school, help you out during an illness, or just someone to pray you through a difficult situation, you can count on your friend.

This week is all about celebrating and being grateful for your relationships, and today is about celebrating friendship. Plan to honor your friend. Treat her to a special lunch, plan a fun day shopping somewhere out of the ordinary, or do something else you know she'll enjoy. As part of your celebration, give your friend a small token of your gratitude that she can carry with her as a reminder of your friendship. It could be something as simple as a polished stone to remind her that she is your rock—strong, solid, and unchanging—or a charm or other small item she can put on her keychain as a reminder that her friendship is important to you.

Edith Wharton said about a lifelong friend, "There is one friend in the life of each of us who seems not a separate person, however dear and beloved, but an expansion, an interpretation, of one's self, the very meaning of one's soul."[14] Maybe you have a friend like that. Treasure her gift of friendship.

---

14   Hermione Lee, *Edith Wharton*, rev. ed. (New York: Vintage Books, 2008), 716.

❧ The Last Word ❧

Have you written this week's scripture verse on your heart? Memorizing scripture can be more fun when you memorize with a friend. Try these techniques:

* *Quiz each other using the memory cards in this book.*
    "What is 1 Thessalonians 1:2?"
    "We give thanks to God always for you all, making
        mention of you in our prayers."
    Or, turn it around:
    "What is 'We give thanks to God always for you all,
        making mention of you in our prayers'?"
    "First Thessalonians 1:2!"

* *Create more memory cards to memorize additional verses.*

* *Repetition helps. With your friend, plan to text a verse to each other from memory three times a day.*

* *Discuss the memory verse. State the verse from memory then share with your friend what it means to you. Say the verse again.*

* *Create a secret phrase to interject into your everyday conversations. When your friend hears you say it, she has to say this week's verse from memory:*
    "Don't forget that we're going shopping on Friday,
        and, by the way, what's the good word?"
    "First Thessalonians 1:2! 'We give thanks to God always
        for you all, making mention of you in our prayers.' "

What other fun ways can you think of to memorize scripture together?

Week 2: DAY FIVE
THOSE WHO SERVE

It's a routine morning. You get the kids out the door just as the school bus pulls up in front of your house. You wave to the driver, and as she closes the door, you trust her to keep your kids safe on the way to school. You know the principal or teachers will be waiting when your kids get off the bus. You get into your car, turn on the radio, and head to work. An announcer on your local station warns about construction on the expressway causing a traffic backup. You're prepared as you ease by the big work machines and the man wearing a neon-green vest and holding a sign that says SLOW. Just beyond the roadwork, a sheriff's vehicle, red lights flashing, has a car pulled over on the shoulder maybe for driving too fast through the construction zone. You exit the expressway onto a city street, yielding for an ambulance and fire truck on their way to help someone somewhere. Finally, you park your car, enter the building where you work, and say, "Good morning," to the security guard in the lobby. Everything is routine, just another ordinary workday. But, what if—

What if the bus driver hadn't shown up? What if you couldn't count on the school's principal and teachers to keep your kids safe? What if no one had warned you of the road construction and eased you through, if there had been no sheriff's deputy watching for unsafe drivers, no firefighters, emergency medical responders, or security guards? Each day, you come across people in your community working to make your life easier and keep you safe. You are surrounded by people who do thankless but important work.

49

They become part of your daily routine.

If you stop to think about it, you'll realize how many people work to make your life better in jobs so routine they go without thanks. Sanitation workers, postal workers, mail carriers, law enforcement, and rescue dispatchers. What about referees who volunteer at your kids' sports events? Table bussers or the teen who packs your groceries in the checkout line?

Your relationships with others extend beyond your inner circle of family, coworkers, and friends. Each day you connect with others in a small and routine way. You might not know their names or anything about them other than they work to serve you and often without thanks.

In his book *Life's Journeys According to Mister Rogers: Things to Remember Along the Way*, the beloved Fred Rogers wrote, "I remember one of my seminary professors saying people who were able to appreciate others—who looked for what was good and healthy and kind—were about as close as you could get to God—to the eternal good."[15] A little appreciation goes a long way. Tomorrow, as you go about your daily routine, recognize those who serve, and thank them. A simple thank-you helps make the world a nicer place.

We give thanks to God always for you all,
making mention of you in our prayers.
1 THESSALONIANS 1:2

.

15   Fred Rogers, *Life's Journeys According to Mister Rogers: Things to Remember Along the Way*, rev. ed. (New York: Hachette Books, 2019).

❧ *The Blank Page* ❧

Fred Rogers also said, "The world needs a sense of worth, and it will achieve it only by its people feeling that they are worthwhile . . . . Try your best to make goodness attractive. That's one of the toughest assignments you'll ever be given."[16]

Your assignment today is to show gratefulness to community helpers. Make it a family affair. Talk with your kids about all the people in their lives whose help might go unnoticed. Decide on ways your family, as individuals and collectively, can show them gratefulness. Here are a few ideas:

Take a treat to the firehouse nearest to your neighborhood.

On a hot day, give a bottle of cold water to the mail carrier.

Encourage your kids to write thank-you notes to helpers at school: teachers, custodians, lunch room helpers, aides, crossing guards, school bus drivers. On trash pickup day, leave a thank-you note on the trash can for the sanitation workers.

At community events where police officers are on duty, if you have the opportunity, take your children to an officer to say hello. You might want to give the officer an inexpensive gift card to a fast-food restaurant or coffee shop as a little token of thanks for keeping you safe.

These acts of gratefulness will not only help others feel worthwhile, but it will make you and your family more aware of the people around you who do important but often thankless jobs.

---

16   Fred Rogers, *You Are Special: Neighborly Words of Wisdom from Mister Rogers,* rev. ed. (New York: Penguin, 1995), 9.

The Last Word

Gratitude inspires good work. Saying "thank you," complimenting, congratulating, and celebrating are key ways to motivate workers to work harder and better. From his study on gratitude, Robert Emmons concluded that gratefulness was an even better motivator than money. In an employee appreciation survey conducted by the job recruitment site Glassdoor, 80 percent of workers said they'd work harder for an appreciative boss, and 70 percent said appreciation in the workplace would make them feel better about themselves and their efforts.

When you offer sincere thanks to people for doing their jobs well, you encourage them. You don't know, but maybe God has led you to a person in a specific moment when he or she is disappointed in their work. Your gratefulness might be just the motivator that person needs to keep going, to keep trying to do their job well.

Every job well done is a job worthy of gratefulness. Whether it is at home or in your workplace, be the person who says "thanks," the one who readily offers compliments, congratulations, and praise. When you show gratitude toward others, it not only makes them feel better; it gives you a happiness boost too! There's nothing quite like the feeling you get when your gratitude makes someone smile.

Week 2: DAY SIX
THE KINDNESS OF STRANGERS

In Matthew, Jesus speaks about the end times, what it will be like for those He will welcome into heaven. He says,

" 'Come, you who have been called by My Father.
Come into the holy nation that has been made ready
for you before the world was made. For I was hungry and
you gave Me food to eat. I was thirsty and you gave Me
water to drink. I was a stranger and you gave Me a room.
I had no clothes and you gave Me clothes to wear.
I was sick and you cared for Me. I was in
prison and you came to see Me.'

"Then those that are right with God will say, 'Lord,
when did we see You hungry and feed You? When did we
see You thirsty and give You a drink? When did we see
You a stranger and give You a room? When did we see
You had no clothes and we gave You clothes? And when
did we see You sick or in prison and we came to You?'
Then the King will say, 'For sure, I tell you, because you
did it to one of the least of My brothers, you have
done it to Me.' " (Matthew 25:34–40 NLV)

Clearly, God wants us to show loving-kindness toward others just as if they were Him. In His speech, Jesus included strangers. Hebrews 13:2 (NLV) reminds us of this: "Do not forget to be kind to strangers. . . . Some people have had angels in their homes without knowing it."

Each day, strangers help in unexpected and spontaneous ways. Their acts are voluntary and genuine. Whether it is something as small as taking our shopping carts to the cart corrals, thereby saving us a few steps, or risking their lives to rescue us from danger, these strangers selflessly do what is good and right as if they were doing it for God. They have nothing to gain and sometimes everything to sacrifice. Often, we don't know their names. They show up to help and then they are gone. We might think of them as angels, God's servants showing up exactly when and where we need them.

Maybe you've been someone's unidentified angel, or maybe you've been on the receiving end of a stranger's kindness. Maybe your helper acted swiftly and then disappeared, leaving you wishing you had offered more thanks. God knows who that person is. He sees His people when they help each other. You can give thanks to Him for those who are ready and willing to help. You can specifically ask Him to bless the unnamed strangers who come to your aid. Then, every day, you can further show your gratitude by paying forward the kindness shown to you. Jesus says, "For sure, I tell you, because you did it to one of the least of My brothers, you have done it to Me" (Matthew 25:40 NLV). When you do for others, you are doing for Him.

We give thanks to God always for you all,
making mention of you in our prayers.
1 THESSALONIANS 1:2

The Blank Page

Keep your eyes open today for strangers performing good deeds. Watch especially for little things: someone holding open a door, retrieving an item on a shelf too high for another to reach, allowing a person with just a few groceries to go ahead in the checkout line—small ways of helping, still significant in God's eyes. Each time you see a stranger do something kind today, say a silent prayer and thank God for that person. Thank Him for the kindness of strangers, not only those who help you but also for strangers helping others.

During a flight in 2018, a Chicago teacher talked to the passenger next to her, a stranger, about challenges she faced working with low-income students. The passenger asked for her contact information, wanting to donate to her school. Another passenger overheard and donated five hundred dollars. Two more passengers donated twenty dollars and ten. "Do something amazing," one of them said. The teacher, overwhelmed by the strangers' kindness, posted about it on Facebook. "I was in complete awe that I had touched a stranger," she wrote. "I want to pass this story around and thank those strangers and their amazing hearts!"

The teacher used social media to thank the strangers in her story. If someone has helped you in an unexpected way and you weren't able to say "thank you," think of other ways you could pass your story around.

The Last Word

What kind of stranger are you? When was the last time you did something considerate, generous, and unexpected for someone you don't know? Every day, you have opportunities to serve God by being a compassionate and caring stranger. By engaging in even the smallest acts of kindness, you help further God's kingdom here on earth.

Thomas Jefferson wrote: "Everything is useful which contributes to fix us in the principles and practice of virtue. When any original act of charity or of gratitude, for instance, is presented either to our sight or imagination, we are deeply impressed with its beauty and feel a strong desire in ourselves of doing charitable and grateful acts also." In other words, kindness is contagious. When we're on the receiving end of kindness, it makes us more likely to pay it forward. Receiving an unexpected act of kindness from a stranger, especially one that goes beyond the ordinary, makes us feel suddenly grateful. It opens our hearts to the goodness in the world and to God's willingness and readiness to meet our needs.

Be a kind stranger, one who provides help to and advocates for others. Be grateful too that God has appointed you His ambassador of kindness to the world.

Week 2: DAY SEVEN
PUTTING IT ALL TOGETHER

This week, you've thought about how you relate to your children, spouse, friends, the people who serve your community, and even strangers. But there's one more relationship to think about—and it's the most important one—your relationship with God.

God has the most thankless job of any. The Creator of the universe, the One who holds the stars in the sky, goes without thanks for most of what He does. When was the last time you thanked Him for each breath you take or each beat of a heart that consistently pumps blood through your body, keeping you alive? For eyes that allow you to read a good book and see your baby's smile? For ears that hear "I love you"? When you wake in the morning, do you thank God that night turned to day or that He watched over you, keeping you safe while you slept unaware? God's never-ending commitment to you, His love, forgiveness, and mercy are the reasons you are here and alive. Your relationship with Him determines where you will spend eternity. He loves you so much that He even sacrificed His Son, Jesus, so you might live with Him forever in heaven. In your daily prayers, do you thank God for Jesus?

Your relationship with God affects every other relationship you have. When you study the Bible and learn what God expects of you in relationships, you are more likely to relate successfully with others. You can be a good influence on them and lead them closer to God. Your relationship with Him guides you through the bad times and provides you with comfort. It helps make you strong and aids you in making right decisions. Your relationship with Him is more important than any other because it is eternal. It began before you were born and will last after you die and forever.

Each day, God performs thankless miracles. We tend to think of miracles as big things. Someone is healed of a terminal disease. A tornado threatening to destroy a small rural town miraculously disappears into the clouds. A child who doctors said would never walk not only walks but runs! Big things. Miracles. But each day the miracle of life itself goes unnoticed. There are endless miracles God does, miracles that give us life, sustain our lives, and provide us with abundant life that are so ubiquitous, we take them for granted. We fail to see them.

In 2 Corinthians 4:18 (CEV), Paul says, "Things that are seen don't last forever, but things that are not seen are eternal. That's why we keep our minds on the things that cannot be seen." Do that today and every day—keep your mind on God and your relationship with Him. Make it your first priority. Open your eyes to the miracles that surround you, and thank God for all the wonderful things He does, especially those you can't see.

We give thanks to God always for you all,
making mention of you in our prayers.
1 THESSALONIANS 1:2

❧ The Blank Page ❧

God created your brain to hold memories. You can imagine your brain as a computer. Some memories are readily available on your "desktop," other files you need to search for, and some even pop up unexpectedly. "Oh, now I remember that file!" When you memorize a scripture verse, it's in your brain. You decide where to store it. You can either put it on your desktop for easy recall or file it away and maybe even forget about it.

Get in the habit of storing scripture on your desktop—front and center in your brain. Think about memory verses often, and apply them to your daily life. Organize scripture in your mind in "folders" by themes so that when you face specific situations, you can open a folder and find the verses you need. Keep in mind that Satan is like a computer virus. He exists to destroy your files. Don't allow it! Be vigilant. Protect your brain with scripture verses that will defeat him better than the best virus protection software.

Have you memorized this week's Bible verse: "We give thanks to God always for you all, making mention of you in our prayers" (1 Thessalonians 1:2)? Pray and ask God to help you memorize scripture. Make His words the first files you open every day.

❧ The Last Word ❧

Dear God, thank You for the special relationships I enjoy with my family and friends. I'm grateful for the love, laughter, and support they give me. Thank You for opening my eyes to those helpers around me doing Your work. Father, You have taught me so much about life and living through the people I've met. I'm grateful to You for those lessons. I'm grateful most of all for the relationship I have with You, the One who holds me close. In those times when I drift away from You and lose sight of Your many blessings, rescue me. Help me to keep my mind fixed on You—the most important One in my life. Amen.

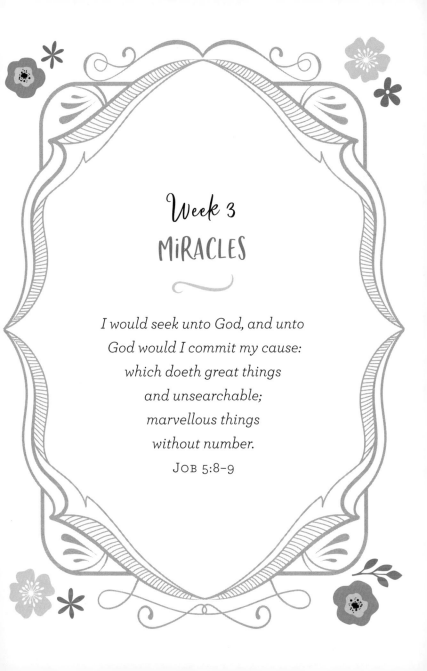

Week 3

MIRACLES

*I would seek unto God, and unto
God would I commit my cause:
which doeth great things
and unsearchable;
marvellous things
without number.*

JOB 5:8-9

MiRACLES

Job suffered all kinds of trouble. He was sick, family members had died, and his herds of animals had died as well. The words of this week's memory verse come from Job's friend Eliphaz, offering advice to Job. He says, "Job, if I were you, I would ask God for help. His miracles are marvelous, more than we can count" (Job 5:8–9 CEV). In Job's state of mind, he likely had trouble seeing God's miracles. But Eliphaz did his best to remind Job that God is in everything and always doing marvelous things.

So much of what God does is unseen. We live on a planet that appears as a tiny speck in a universe so big it's beyond our imaginations; still, God cares about us. He is responsible for the air we breathe that keeps us alive, the gravity that holds us here, the energy around us, the radio waves that bring information and entertainment. We can't see our thoughts, our feelings, or our souls, but, thanks to God, they are there. Unseen things. God's miracles. Marvelous things.

In his poem "Miracles," Walt Whitman wrote:

Why, who makes much of a miracle?
As to me I know of nothing else but miracles,
Whether I walk the streets of Manhattan,
Or dart my sight over the roofs of houses toward the sky,
Or wade with naked feet along the beach
just in the edge of the water,
Or stand under trees in the woods,
Or talk by day with any one I love, or sleep in

the bed at night with any one I love,
Or sit at table at dinner with the rest,

Or look at strangers opposite me riding in the car,
Or watch honey-bees busy around the hive of a summer forenoon,
Or animals feeding in the fields,
Or birds, or the wonderfulness of insects in the air,
Or the wonderfulness of the sundown,
or of stars shining so quiet and bright,
Or the exquisite delicate thin curve of the new moon in spring;
These with the rest, one and all, are to me miracles,
The whole referring, yet each distinct and in its place.

To me every hour of the light and dark is a miracle,
Every cubic inch of space is a miracle,
Every square yard of the surface of the
earth is spread with the same,
Every foot of the interior swarms with the same.
To me the sea is a continual miracle,
The fishes that swim—the rocks—the motion of the waves—
the ships with men in them,
What stranger miracles are there?

Whitman's words remind us that there are big miracles, small miracles, obvious miracles, and miracles we cannot see. God is all around us doing marvelous things. This week we'll take a look at some of them and discover even more reasons to give thanks to God.

I would seek unto God, and unto God would I commit my
cause: which doeth great things and unsearchable;
marvellous things without number.

JOB 5:8-9

63

What is a miracle? Lexico, the Oxford University Press (previously the Oxford Dictionary), offers three definitions:

1. "A surprising and welcome event that is not explicable by natural or scientific laws and is therefore considered to be the work of a divine agency."

There are many Bible examples of this kind of miracle: Shadrach, Meshach, and Abednego escaping death in a fiery furnace, Jesus healing the sick, Sarah conceiving a child in her old age. Can you think of one modern-day miracle to fit this definition?

2. "A highly improbable or extraordinary event, development, or accomplishment that brings very welcome consequences."

An example: It was a miracle when the US men's hockey team won a gold medal in the 1980 Winter Olympics. List several other examples.

3. "An amazing product or achievement, or an outstanding example of something."[17]

There are plenty of examples fitting this third definition. Add to your list three products that you couldn't live without.

God (a divine agency) is only mentioned in the first of Oxford's definitions, but Psalm 24:1 (NLV) tells us: "The earth is the Lord's, and all that is in it, the world, and all who live in it." Every example you can think of that fits these three definitions is made possible by God. Think about that today, and give thanks to God.

---

17   Lexico, s.v. "miracle," https://www.lexico.com/definition/miracle.

❧ The Last Word ❧

When trying to memorize longer scripture verses, our minds sometimes want to change the order of the words, insert words that are not there, or even delete words. One way to avoid this is to break the verse into easy-to-remember parts.

1. Memorize the scripture reference. Say it often: "Job 5:8–9."

2. After you have memorized the reference, find the book of Job in your Bible. Then look up Job 5:8–9 and read it aloud. "I would seek unto God, and unto God would I commit my cause: which doeth great things and unsearchable; marvellous things without number."

3. Decide how you can break the passage into memory parts:

   ❋ *"I would seek unto God,*

   ❋ *and unto God would I commit my cause:*

   ❋ *which doeth great things and unsearchable;*

   ❋ *marvellous things without number."*

4. Memorize each part separately until you've memorized the entire verse.

The term for breaking tasks into smaller parts is *microprogress*. Breaking scripture into parts makes the memory task more approachable. If you dread anything that requires a lot of memorization, breaking the task into small parts helps keep you motivated so you can continue working toward your goal.

Week 3: DAY TWO
GODWINKS!

Dictionaries regularly add new words and expressions. Have you heard of *Godwink*? It's a term invented by author SQuire Rushnell in his book *When God Winks: How the Power of Coincidence Guides Your Life*. "A Godwink," he says, "is a personal signal or message directly from a higher power, usually but not always, in the form of a coincidence."[18] The term might be new, but Godwinks have always existed. When an inconvenience or change in routine leads someone to be in the right place at the right time, it's a Godwink.

An author friend tells of the day she was so ill on a flight to a writer's conference that she almost got off the plane at a layover. She nearly contacted a friend to take the session she was scheduled to teach at the conference. But she began to feel better and traveled on. It was at the conference that the author met her future husband. "Thank God I felt better," she said, "or we might never have met." Godwink!

Many examples of Godwinks exist during the events of September 11, 2001, the day of the terrorist attacks in New York City and Washington, DC. A shirt the wearer felt clashed with his necktie led him back to his hotel room to change. He was scheduled to speak at a meeting in the Twin Towers, and had it not been for the necktie change, he would have been on the 104th floor of the North Tower when the plane hit. Thank God, his life was spared. A New York Giants' game that went late into the night of September 10th

---

18   Squire Rushnell, *When God Winks: How the Power of Coincidence Guides Your Life* (Brentwood, TN: Howard Books, 2002).

caused several people to oversleep on the morning of September 11th. Late for work, they escaped being in the towers when the planes hit. A chef at the Windows on the World restaurant, at the top of the North Tower, stopped on his way to work to pick up a new pair of eyeglasses. Had it not been for a change in routine, he would have been in the restaurant and died on that fateful day. Godwinks!

"There but for the grace of God go I" is an expression attributed to sixteenth-century clergyman John Bradford. He said it when his life was spared among martyrs being led to the gallows. It reminds us there are no coincidences, only Godwinks—acts of God's grace. All of us are recipients of God's goodness, kindness, and love.

"Thank God." It's something we say often. God's grace is everywhere all the time providing us with reasons to thank Him. Proverbs 19:21 (NLV) tells us, "There are many plans in a [person's] heart, but it is the Lord's plan that will stand." God is always winking at us, making us aware of His presence in ways big and small, saving us from consequences beyond our imaginations, or leading us unexpectedly down a new road toward something good. Thank God for His Godwinks. Thank God for His overwhelming and abundant grace.

I would seek unto God, and unto God would I commit my
cause: which doeth great things and unsearchable;
marvellous things without number.

JOB 5:8–9

❧ The Blank Page ❧

The great mystery author Agatha Christie said, "Any coincidence is worth noticing." Are you good at observation? Do you notice when God winks? Think about times you've been on the receiving end of a Godwink, something unexplainable that led you down His path instead of your own. Here are five questions to consider:

1. Did a chance meeting guide you into a new and lasting relationship?
2. Has a loss (being downsized from your job, for example) led you to something better?
3. In a time of need, did someone suddenly show up to help you?
4. Have you rekindled a relationship after you unexpectedly ran into an old acquaintance?
5. Did an item you lost and treasured somehow find its way back to you?

What about life-saving or life-altering Godwinks—the really big things that changed you forever? Maybe a change in routine saved your life, or maybe God led you to a business idea that resulted in financial security. Maybe you discovered a new medication or procedure that significantly improved your quality of life, or after years of feeling lonely, you finally met and married the love of your life. Did you always know God, or did something unexpected lead you to Him?

Keep your eyes open for all the little and big Godwinks around you. Every minute of every day, through His grace He is guiding your steps and blessing you with new possibilities.

The Last Word

You can't read the Bible without noticing the Godwinks—God leading His people to be in just the right places at the right times. Think of Joseph's story. He brought his jealous brothers food while they were tending their flocks of sheep. Just then, merchants showed up willing to buy and sell Joseph as a slave. As a result, Joseph became second in command to Pharaoh and saved the Israelites from starvation.

In Esther's story, was it a coincidence that Mordecai overheard the king's officers plotting to kill the king? That resulted not only in saving the king's life but also the lives of all the Jews in his kingdom.

Was it a coincidence that Ruth decided to stay with her mother-in-law, Naomi, and travel with her to Bethlehem? That decision led Ruth to meet her future husband, Boaz. They married and had a son, Obed, who grew up to be the father of Jesse, who would become the father of King David.

Luke 7:1–10 tells the story of a centurion whose beloved servant was sick and near death. Was it a coincidence that Jesus just happened to be nearby and healed the servant?

God says, "I am the Lord your God. . .Who leads you in the way you should go" (Isaiah 48:17 NLV). There are no coincidences, just incidences of God leading us and guiding our steps according to His plans.

Week 3: DAY THREE
THROUGH A CHILD'S EYES

Before eating their Thanksgiving meals, some families practice the tradition of each person at the table saying what he or she is grateful for. Adults are thankful for family, love, life, friends, God. . .but children have other unusual reasons to be thankful. In their innocence, they are more aware of little things adults might not notice or take for granted. When asked what they were thankful for, some kids responded: "Ceiling fans, toilet paper, snowmen, corn (because it tastes better than broccoli), the Statue of Liberty (because she's pretty), gas! (the kind that makes a car run), chocolate chip cookies, quesadillas, peanut butter and jelly, dinosaurs, mermaids, animals (except sharks that bite and "flying mice"—bats), sprinkles, rainbows, sunshine, stars. . ." Real answers from real kids.

A miracle can be "an amazing product or achievement, or an outstanding example of something." For children, colorful little candies sprinkled on cupcakes is an amazing product, a miracle. It's a great achievement to shape snow into the form of a man, woman, or anything else, another miracle. Corn is an outstanding example of a vegetable that's tasty and worthy of praise. A miracle.

Children are thankful for simple things, everyday things. We can learn much about gratefulness when we see miracles through their humble, innocent eyes. Kids recognize God's existence in rainbows, sunshine, and stars. To them, caterpillars turning into butterflies and seeds becoming plants that produce vegetables and flowers are miracles. So are kittens, puppies, and babies. It's a miracle that a brother or sister is a nice sibling and not a monster that hides under their bed (another reason for gratefulness offered by a child at the Thanksgiving table).

We can learn even more about miracles and gratefulness by listening to a child's bedtime prayers. "Thank You, God, that I didn't throw up in school today. . .thank You that Daddy didn't have to work tonight and came to my ball game. . .thank You for my dog and my friends, and for reminding me not to leave my backpack at school again. . .thank You for mint chocolate chip ice cream!"

True gratefulness comes when we see God's grace, His kindness extended to us in the smallest, most insignificant things. We wake up every morning; we have clothing to wear, clean water to bathe in, food to eat, transportation to work or school. We have family and friends who love us, people we can rely on. God's hand can be seen in all the little miracles: the products we use, the things we achieve, the amazing examples of things that motivate us and make us more aware of God's presence.

Kailash Satyarthi, winner of the Nobel Peace Prize in 2014 said, "Childhood means simplicity. Look at the world with the child's eye—it is very beautiful."[19] Think about that. What beautiful things might you discover today if you viewed the world through the eyes of a child?

I would seek unto God, and unto God would I commit my cause: which doeth great things and unsearchable; marvellous things without number.

JOB 5:8-9

---

19   Kailash Satyarthi, AZ Quotes, https://www.azquotes.com/quote/1122355.

❧ The Blank Page ❧

Here's a game you can play with a young child. Take turns saying something you are thankful for. Keep going until one of you runs out of ideas. Dig deeper into gratefulness by asking for reasons.

Child: "I'm grateful for my body."

You: "Why?"

Child: "Because it moves."

Children have a way of paring things down into their simplest form, the essence of gratefulness. An adult might express thanks for how complex the human body is and its parts that work together with precise timing to sustain life, but a child thinks of the human body and is grateful just because it moves. It's enough for him or her in that moment, one simple present reason to be grateful.

Try your best to look at the world sometimes through the eyes of children. Throw out the big ideas for a while and concentrate on what's simple. The Bible tells us in Psalm 116:6 (NKJV): "The LORD preserves the simple." Open your eyes and your heart to the many ways God extends His grace to you through little blessings. Don't overlook the simple things in everyday life. Miracles are hidden there, but you might only see them if you look through the eyes of a child.

The Last Word

Many of the poems in Robert Louis Stevenson's *A Child's Garden of Verses* are examples of how children notice details and see the extraordinary in everyday things. For example, his poem "The Cow":

The friendly cow all red and white,
I love with all my heart:
She gives me cream with all her might...
And blown by all the winds that pass
And wet with all the showers,
She walks among the meadow grass
And eats the meadow flowers.

And his poem "Escape at Bedtime" about a child observing the stars:

The lights from the parlor and kitchen shone out
Through the blinds and the windows and bars;
And high overhead and all moving about,
There were thousands of millions of stars.
There ne'er were such thousands of leaves on a tree,
Nor of people in church or the Park,
As the crowds of the stars that looked down upon me,
And that glittered and winked in the dark...
They saw me at last, and they chased me with cries,
And they soon had me packed into bed;
But the glory kept shining and bright in my eyes,
And the stars going round in my head.

Try to think like the children in Stevenson's poems. Find the beauty in the smallest details in everyday things then offer your thanks to God.

Week 3: DAY FOUR
EPIC MIRACLES

Epic. You can't say the word without thinking big. *Epic* calls up images of mammoth waves, huge crowds, and movies like *Ben Hur* and *The Ten Commandments.* "Epic" fits the definition of a miracle that says: "a surprising and welcome event that is not explicable by natural or scientific laws and is therefore considered to be the work of a divine agency."

The Bible is filled with epic miracles.

In Exodus 14, you can read about Moses leading thousands of Israelites out of slavery in Egypt. God in a pillar of fire and cloud went ahead of them. Pharaoh's army pursued them, all of his horses, chariots, and soldiers. When the Israelites found themselves trapped between the Red Sea and Pharaoh's army, God told Moses to stretch out his hand toward the water. When he did, the sea parted. The Israelites walked on a dry path with the water forming walls to their left and right. When the Israelites were safe on the other side, God closed the sea, and it swallowed Pharaoh's army. Epic miracle—and an epic reason for the Israelites to be thankful.

This was just the beginning of the miracles God would perform as the Israelites traveled to their new home. When they wandered through the desert, God provided food—manna, a bread-like substance that fell from the sky. A large flock of quails came into their camp out of nowhere. A rock produced water when Moses struck it with his walking stick.

On Mount Sinai, God gave Moses the Ten Commandments. He

told Moses, "I promise to perform miracles for you that have never been seen anywhere on earth. Neighboring nations will stand in fear and know that I was the one who did these marvelous things" (Exodus 34:10 CEV).

The Israelites had already seen God perform epic miracles, and more were on the way. They had epic reasons to be grateful, but instead they complained. When Moses was delayed coming back from the mountain, the Israelites lost their faith. They built an idol, a statue of a golden calf. They bowed to it, sacrificed to it, and said, "This is the god who brought us out of Egypt!" (Exodus 32:4 CEV). You might say it was an epic fail. Still, God in His mercy continued performing miracles.

God performs miracles today, although some might argue not big miracles like those in the Bible. Like the Israelites, we complain when we can't see God, or we lose faith when His timing isn't in sync with ours. Still, His mercy surrounds us. We can't know as we go about our daily routines what miracles God is working in the background to save us from danger, sickness, and evil. But He is there.

The same God who did those epic miracles for the Israelites is caring for you right now. So, honor Him. Be grateful. Thank Him today for His commitment to you and His unfailing and never-ending love.

I would seek unto God, and unto God would I commit my cause: which doeth great things and unsearchable; marvellous things without number.

JOB 5:8-9

The Blank Page

This week's memory verse is a reminder that God does great things that are unsearchable, marvelous, and immeasurable. Some of His work fits another definition of "miracle": "a highly improbable or extraordinary event, development, or accomplishment that brings very welcome consequences."

Today, consider some of the best moments of your life. Did something good happen that was highly improbable or extraordinary? Did you accomplish something you never thought you would? Write down at least one example from

* *your early childhood*
* *your school days*
* *when you were a young adult*
* *the past year*

Next, jot down and complete these sentences:

The best thing that ever happened to me was _____.

My greatest accomplishment was _____.

The most extraordinary thing God has done for me is

_____.

The things you've written are examples of the miraculous ways God has worked in your life. He's constantly leading and guiding you. What epic thing might you experience or accomplish next? God knows, but you can only imagine.

The Last Word

It's time to review this week's memory verse: "I would seek unto God, and unto God would I commit my cause: which doeth great things and unsearchable; marvellous things without number" (Job 5:8–9).

Are you using the scripture memory cards that come with this book? Remember to make them part of your daily routine. Put the card on your bathroom mirror, and practice the scripture while you do your hair and makeup. Take the card with you. Put it where you can see it throughout the day. Prioritize memorizing the scripture; make it the first item on your to-do list. At bedtime, recite the scripture to God in prayer, and ask Him to help you apply it to your life.

Stock up on 3x5 note cards. They can be bought inexpensively at dollar stores. Note cards are great for memorizing longer scripture verses. Write each word of the verse on a separate card. Then put the cards in order. This helps train your brain not only to put the words in the correct order but also to visualize the verse.

Week 3: DAY FIVE
YOUR AMAZING BODY

The Bible says God creates us. He makes our body parts and puts them together inside our mothers' wombs (Psalm 139:13). Even before we are born, God gives our bodies everything they need to live. He creates within us countless tiny miracles. Scientists have discovered some of them, but the rest are God's secrets.

We know that our bodies contain about seven billion billion billion atoms, and inside each atom are even smaller parts: protons, neutrons, and electrons. Our bodies have the same genes arranged in the same order. Most of our DNA is the same too, but God created just enough differences to make each of us unique.

He created our hearts to be complex machines with perfectly coordinating parts. The right side pumps blood into the lungs. The left side pumps it back into the body. Every minute our hearts pump 1½ gallons of blood, beating on average one hundred thousand times a day.

We need oxygen to live, and God created a way for it to enter our bodies. When we breathe in, oxygen goes into the lungs and is absorbed by blood, which carries it to all our cells, tissues, and organs. Cells use the oxygen and create carbon dioxide, which the blood carries back to our lungs and is removed when we exhale. This happens, on average, between twelve and twenty times a minute from the moment we are born till the moment we die.

The brain, the central processing unit of our existence, receives and processes information from our bodies and from external sources. Our brains send signals to our bodies to regulate functions like breathing, heartbeat, and blood pressure. Brains hold all our memories. They are like computers, constantly storing data, only they are far more complex than any computer on earth. God controls the data in our brains and distributes it to us as needed.

Scientists don't fully understand the body and everything the brain can do, but God does. There's nothing about our bodies and about us that He doesn't understand. He is our Creator, the One in control.

In Psalm 139:1–4 (NLV), David says, "O Lord, You have looked through me and have known me. You know when I sit down and when I get up. You understand my thoughts from far away. You look over my path and my lying down. You know all my ways very well. Even before I speak a word, O Lord, You know it all." God does know it all! He is responsible for our existence and the miracles that allow our bodies to live and our brains to think. He adds the miracle of giving us souls, an unseen and mysterious part known only to Him, the part that allows us to live on even after our bodies die.

Give thanks today to God, your Creator.

"Thank you [dear Lord] for making me so wonderfully complex! Your workmanship is marvelous—how well I know it" (Psalm 139:14 NLT).

I would seek unto God, and unto God would I commit my cause: which doeth great things and unsearchable; marvellous things without number.

JOB 5:8–9

Pay closer attention to your body and the signals it could be sending you. Get into the habit of knowing yourself inside and out. Remember that God is in control of your body's data, and He knows everything that's going on. If you feel tired often, for example, it might be God trying to communicate that you need more sleep or wanting you to examine your priorities and slow down a bit, or He could be guiding you toward a checkup with your doctor.

Whenever you feel a little off, think about why you might feel that way. Spend time with the Lord in prayer and ask Him to lead you. Maybe you are just having a bad day and all you require is an attitude adjustment. On the other hand, that off feeling could be God's way of making you aware that something needs attention. Remember, you are the caretaker of the body God gave you. If that off feeling persists, don't just assume that everything is fine, and don't let fear stop you from seeking help. Your Creator wants you to take care of His creation. Center yourself in His love and trust Him to guide you.

The Last Word

Ten Tips for Staying Healthy

1. Learn about healthy eating. Prepare nutritious meals for yourself and your family.

2. Get moving. Make exercise part of your daily routine. Even modest amounts of exercise can do a world of good.

3. Watch your weight. Avoid fast-food meals and unhealthy snacks, and be aware of your portions.

4. Avoid alcohol and quit smoking. These habits put you at higher risk for cancer, heart disease, and strokes.

5. Learn to deal with stress. Instead of allowing it to build up inside you, remember you can give it to God. There's nothing He can't handle.

6. Get enough sleep. Your cell phone and other smart devices need recharging—and so do you!

7. Drink plenty of water. It keeps you hydrated and helps maintain the balance of your body fluids.

8. Maintain a positive attitude. Staying positive helps you to be happy and to cope with life's challenges.

9. Wash your hands, and wash them well. It's one of the easiest and most effective ways of stopping germs that can make you sick.

10. Get regular checkups. Catch problems early, and stay on top of vaccinations and routine tests.

Week 3: DAY Six
INSTINCT

Two opposite forces work within us: impulse and instinct. One is from God and the other is not. A child takes a cookie after his mother tells him not to. "I don't know why I did it," he says. "I just did." That's impulse. It's giving in to an urge without thinking it through. Impulse is exercising our own will. In contrast, a hero runs into a burning building and comes out with a child safely cradled in his arms. "I don't know why I went in," he says. "I just did." That's instinct. It's God sparing us from thinking something through and instead sending a message directly to our brains, causing us to act according to His will.

If you take time to observe animals, you'll notice many examples of instinctive behavior. Spiders spin webs instinctively. No one teaches them to do it. Birds build nests, caterpillars make cocoons, baby ducks follow their mother, bears hibernate through winter—all are examples of God sending a direct message that results in a specific act. A tiny newborn kangaroo, the size of a jelly bean, knows to crawl from its mother's womb up her body to the safety of her pouch. When a honeybee dies in the hive, a worker bee knows to remove the corpse. Male animals perform courtship dances to attract the opposite sex. Instinct is God's will implanted in nature. We can see the miracle of Him communicating directly with animals, guiding them without any instruction.

Instinct is also God's gift to us. It is His way of grabbing our hands and pulling us forward without saying to us, "Let's go." It's God wrapping His arms around us from behind and stopping us from walking into danger without telling us, "Watch out!" Instinct is how God guides us. Before we can form our own thoughts, He is there. He doesn't tell us what to do and allow us time to think, but instead He moves quickly, pushing us in the way we should go. Instinct doesn't allow time to feel or think—it just is. It's evidence of God's willingness to protect and sustain us.

Gratitude is an instinct we are born with. Like fear, happiness, shame, and all our other emotions, gratitude can lie dormant until something sparks it. Usually God is the spark. He sends a direct message to us, triggering a feeling of gratitude. How we act on it is a matter of our will. We rarely pray, "Thank You, God, for instincts," yet without them, we wouldn't know to jump out of harm's way or to love or even to want to live. Newborn babies wouldn't know to cry when they need something, and mothers wouldn't intuitively know how to help them.

Thank God for instincts, those miraculous, quick, and unexplainable messages that cause us to act in harmony with His will. They are absolute proof that God exists and that He loves and cares for us.

I would seek unto God, and unto God would I commit my
cause: which doeth great things and unsearchable;
marvellous things without number.

Job 5:8–9

The Blank Page

Instinct is an involuntary force that drives us toward specific activities. We've defined it here as something you do without thinking. Reflexes, for example, are instinctive behaviors. You slip on the ice and grab on to something to break your fall. No one told you what to do. You didn't have to learn to catch yourself. You just instinctively reached out. It's a behavior God planted in you, ready when you need it.

You instinctively blink your eyes, react to sounds, and avoid obstacles in your way. You react instinctively with facial expressions that convey happiness, anger, pain, and fear. Crying when something sad happens in a movie, book, or television show might be one of your instinctive behaviors. You have talents and skills that are innate. You didn't have to learn them. They've always been a part of you. You perform them instinctively.

As you go about your day today, be aware of the things you do that are not thought out, planned, or learned behaviors but result in something good. Also be aware of instinctive behaviors that keep you safe. As you notice these things, you will discover even more reasons to be grateful to God.

The Bible says, "A man's heart plans his way, but the LORD directs his steps" (Proverbs 16:9 NKJV).

❧ The Last Word ❧

"Who has given wisdom to the heart? Who has given understanding to the mind?" (Job 38:36 NLV). This is God speaking to Job. He says, "[The ostrich] leaves her eggs to the earth and lets them get warm in the dust. She forgets that a foot might crush them, or that the wild animal may step on them. . . . Her work of giving birth is for nothing, for she does not care. Because God has not given her wisdom or her share of understanding" (Job 39:14–17 NLV).

God continues, questioning Job: "Do you give the horse his strength? . . . Do you make him jump like the locust? . . . He hits his foot against the ground in the valley. . . . He laughs at fear and is not afraid. . . . He cannot stand still at the sound of the horn. . . . Is it by your understanding that the hawk flies, spreading his wings toward the south? Is it because the eagle is obeying you that he flies high and makes his nest in a high place? He lives on a high rock. His strong place is on the mountain-top that is hard to reach. From there he looks for his food. His eyes see it from far away" (Job 39:19–22, 24, 26–29 NLV).

God provides Job with many examples of the instinctive behavior He is responsible for and the ways He controls the universe. Read more about it in your Bible in Job 38–39.

Throughout this week, you've explored miracles in different forms: epic miracles—surprising and welcome events not explicable by natural or scientific law; Godwinks—highly improbable or extraordinary events, developments, or accomplishments that bring welcome consequences; and miracles that are connected to amazing products, achievements, or outstanding examples. At the beginning of the week, you read Psalm 24:1 (NLV): "The earth is the Lord's, and all that is in it, the world, and all who live in it"—a reminder that every miracle is made possible by God.

Where you saw a coincidence in the past, now you might say it was a miracle. If you played the "I'm thankful" game with a child, maybe you discovered some new miracles to be grateful for. And if you tried to see life through the eyes of a child, you certainly discovered miracles in unlikely places. You explored a few epic miracles from the Bible and examined epic moments in your own life that you know were orchestrated by God. You examined your physical body too and discovered it is made up of a whole string of miracles. You are a miracle! You've thought about instinctive behavior and learned it is from God.

Your entire outlook on miracles might have changed this week.

Albert Einstein is quoted as saying, "There are two ways to live: as though nothing is a miracle, or as though everything is a miracle." Even having said that, Einstein believed, like others today, that God is one with the universe, but He isn't interested in human affairs. Christians believe otherwise: God is the Creator of the universe, and He is not only interested in human affairs, but He loves, guides, and cares for us. Everything is a miracle created by Him.

In Psalm 77:14 (NIV), David praises God, saying, "You are the God who performs miracles; you display your power among the peoples." Have you praised God for His miracles? Have you thanked Him? The Bible tells us to "remember the wonders [God] has done, his miracles, and the judgments he pronounced" (1 Chronicles 16:12 NIV). Job 5:9 (NIV) says, "[God] performs wonders that cannot be fathomed, miracles that cannot be counted." Each day, all around you, there are miracles. You see them in your own life and in the lives of family members, friends, strangers, and even in the animal kingdom. That you are alive is a miracle. The sun rising and setting, the moon, stars, and whatever lies beyond them that you can't see are miracles. How your body was created and is kept alive is evidence of God and His handiwork. The inventions you rely on were made possible by a God-given idea. Some of those inventions might have changed your life in a miraculous way. It's a miracle when you accomplish things you never thought possible.

So many miracles and so many reasons to give thanks!

I would seek unto God, and unto God would I commit my cause: which doeth great things and unsearchable; marvellous things without number.

JOB 5:8–9

The Blank Page

Why is it important to memorize scripture? "Everything in the Scriptures is God's Word. All of it is useful for teaching and helping people and for correcting them and showing them how to live" (2 Timothy 3:16–17 CEV). "God's Word is living and powerful" (Hebrews 4:12 NLV). God's Word is like a lamp that lights our way wherever we walk (Psalm 119:105). Recalling scripture from memory can provide you with strength, comfort, and even the power to be brave in the worst of situations.

In 2011, eighteen-year-old Will Norton was in the car with his father on his way home from his high school graduation. Tornado sirens blared, and Will and his dad drove into the path of a vicious storm. Their car was picked up and tossed like a toy. Will's father remembers Will praying and quoting scripture before, sadly, Will was sucked out of the car and died. In that terrible moment, the Bible verses Will had memorized sustained him. He knew God was there with him.[20]

Have you added this week's Bible verse to those you've memorized? "I would seek unto God, and unto God would I commit my cause: which doeth great things and unsearchable; marvellous things without number" (Job 5:8–9).

If you found yourself in a life-threatening situation like the Nortons, which scripture verses could you rely on?

---

20   Karl Torp, "Joplin Father Remembers Son Killed in Massive Tornado," May 21, 2012, News 9, https://www.news9.com/story/18578156/joplin-father-recalls-massive-tornado-that-killed-teen-age-son.

The Last Word

God of all blessings, thank You for the miracles that surround me. My eyes are open to them. I'm grateful for the small things, the unseen things, the things I take for granted: every beat of my heart, every breath I take, and those things I do instinctively because You are thinking for me and guiding me. I appreciate even more now the conveniences I use every day, inventions born of ideas inspired by You. I'm grateful for those happy little surprises You have given me that I've called "coincidences." My life is a miracle. Everything is a miracle! I am filled with awe at Your wonders morning, noon, and night. Amen.

Week 4
SEASONS

*Unto thee, O God, do we give
thanks, unto thee do we give thanks:
for that thy name is near thy
wondrous works declare.*

PSALM 75:1

Week 4: DAY ONE
SEASONS

The things we are grateful for shift with the seasons of our lives. When we were children, we were thankful for things like toys, crayons, and giraffes at the zoo. In our teen years, we put away our toys and instead were grateful for friends, boyfriends, good grades, and the independence that came with driving a car. As young adults with more responsibility, our thankfulness grows exponentially. The start of a career, a new marriage, the birth of our children, these become key reasons to be grateful, and with each passing year, we add more things to our gratefulness list: solid relationships, good health, new possibilities. . . .

Ecclesiastes 3:1 says that everything on earth has its own time and season. This week, we'll explore not only seasons of the year but also the seasons of life. You'll discover God's grace in each and find even more reasons to be grateful.

Close your eyes for a moment and imagine a big tree with a wide trunk and branches reaching outward and upward. In which season did you imagine the tree? Maybe you imagined it in springtime covered with flowers or tiny, bright green buds. Or maybe your tree wore a heavy shroud of leaves providing shade on a hot summer day. Did you imagine the tree in autumn either dressed in brilliant colors or shedding its leaves? Maybe you saw it in winter with its branches coated with snow and standing strong against the frigid north wind. A tree's appearance changes with the seasons, but one thing remains the same—its roots, the very source of its being. It was from a single seed the roots formed, and then a trunk and branches and leaves. As it matured, the tree became strong, its life sustained through all the seasons thanks to its roots.

God planted the seed that became you. He is the root of your existence. Through each season of your life, He will be with you, blessing you, providing for you, and bringing you through all kinds of weather. In Him, you will remain strong.

This week's memory verse, Psalm 75:1, says, "Unto thee, O God, do we give thanks, unto thee do we give thanks: for that thy name is near thy wondrous works declare." The verse is a song written by a man named Asaph, one of the leaders of David's choir. It is a praise chorus similar to those we sing in churches today.

> *Our God, we thank you*
> *for being so near to us!*
> *Everyone celebrates*
> *your wonderful deeds.* (Psalm 75:1 CEV)

Whichever season of life you are in right now, you have reasons to sing praises to God and to celebrate the ways He works in your life. You have so much to look forward to—happy surprises, new experiences, opportunities, friendships. God isn't done with you yet. Like the tree in your imagination, you still have some growing to do.

Unto thee, O God, do we give thanks, unto thee do we give thanks:
for that thy name is near thy wondrous works declare.

PSALM 75:1

The Blank Page

Think about how your perception of gratitude has changed through the seasons of your life. These questions will guide you.

- *As you've gotten older, have you become more appreciative of people, events, and situations that have shaped you into the person you are today?*

- *Can you look at past seasons and see times when you should have been more grateful?*

- *Is there something you can do now to express gratitude to someone who helped you in the past?*

- *Thinking about the challenges you have faced in life so far, can you find reasons to be grateful? Have those challenges helped you in a positive way?*

- *Has the way you express gratitude changed through the seasons of your life?*

- *Have you discovered that, as your gratitude matured, it deepened your relationship with God?*

- *Which season of life do you consider yourself to be in right now?*

- *What three things are you most grateful for? Are those things different from your previous life seasons?*

- *What is the most important thing you have learned about gratitude?*

Gratitude is the lens through which we view life in a more positive way. It is the vehicle that moves us forward. It changes our attitude, the way we relate to others, and the way we relate to God. Gratitude changes everything!

❧ The Last Word ❧

Put this week's memory card where you can see it: on your desk, your car's dashboard, or on your bathroom mirror. Use it not only as a memory tool but also as a reminder that God is with you all the time, today, tomorrow, and in every season of life. If you work at a desk, He is in the chair next to you. When you walk, He is walking with you every step of the way. When you drive your car, God is with you in the passenger seat. Talk with Him and listen to Him speak to your heart. If you are led into an uncomfortable situation, God is there. He will guide your actions and your words. If fear enters your heart, remember God is bigger than fear. He is huge, powerful, and able to reshape fear into faith. Even before you were born, God was with you, and He will be your constant companion forever.

Week 4: DAY TWO
SPRING

Oh, give us pleasure in the flowers to-day;
And give us not to think so far away
As the uncertain harvest; keep us here
All simply in the springing of the year.[21]

These words are the first stanza of Robert Frost's poem "A Prayer in Spring." They remind us to live in the moment and not leap ahead worrying about what might happen tomorrow. With each sunrise, God provides us a new beginning. He allows us to trust Him in the moment and to lead us through whatever the day holds. He says, "Behold, I make all things new" (Revelation 21:5). "I am about to do something new. See, I have already begun! Do you not see it?" (Isaiah 43:19 NLT).

Do you not see it? In nature, with a spring sunrise, the birds create a symphony. There is a name for it: "the dawn chorus." Cardinals sing *cheer-cheer-cheer* from their perches in trees. Other species join in: robins, warblers, chickadees, thrushes. . . . What a sweet sound to wake up to! Step outside, and you'll notice the fresh, soft scent of the earth waking from its winter sleep. Look up, and you'll see the willows and silver maples adorned with tiny buds. Look down, and you might spot a squirrel or two poking around tree trunks hoping for a taste of oozing sap. If your mind is set on tomorrow, you'll surely miss signs of spring.

Every morning of every day can be like waking up to a dawn chorus and a beautiful spring sunrise. If you awake with anticipation

---

21   Robert Frost, "A Prayer in Spring," Poets.org, https://poets.org/poem/prayer-spring.

that God will bless you throughout the day, you are off to a good start. If you trust Him to lead you, you won't be worried about where you are going or what tomorrow will bring. If you enter each new day with an awareness of God's presence, He will open your senses to all the new things He is doing in your life.

Spring is a perfect time to practice gratitude. In this season of renewal and growth, you can choose to refresh your outlook and be grateful for what is now, in the moment. As time moves you from one minute to the next, you can move with it, appreciating what each new minute holds. You can choose to see God consistently at work in your life. Like a gardener in springtime, He has cleaned up any mess from the last season and is creating an environment for new growth to flourish.

Thank God for new beginnings, for giving you opportunities to change and grow, to do things over, learn from the past, and make things right. Thank God that you are alive today and that even if today isn't the best day ever, tomorrow is coming. The Bible tells us, "The faithful love of the LORD never ends! His mercies never cease. Great is his faithfulness; his mercies begin afresh each morning" (Lamentations 3:22–23 NLT).

Unto thee, O God, do we give thanks, unto thee do we give thanks:
for that thy name is near thy wondrous works declare.

PSALM 75:1

The Blank Page

Are you holding on to something that's keeping you stuck in the past? Without letting go, it can be difficult to move forward and appreciate what God is doing in the present.

God says, "I am about to do something new. See, I have already begun! Do you not see it? I will make a pathway through the wilderness. I will create rivers in the dry wasteland" (Isaiah 43:19 NLT). Read those last two sentences again. God doesn't say, "I can." He says, "I will." If you trust God to lead you forward, He will bring you through the wilderness and to His river of peace.

You can move toward a new beginning by practicing the four Ps.

1. Pray. Ask God to lead you forward and rid you from pain, shame, or whatever negative feelings you hold on to from the past.

2. Pardon. Forgive yourself and others for past transgressions. This doesn't mean forgetting what happened, or the pain it caused you, or allowing yourself to stay in a bad situation. It means learning to live with what happened without bitterness or hatred.

3. Pacify. Soothe your anger, agitation, or sorrow by reading God's Word and trusting in the Lord's loving-kindness.

4. Persevere. Keep going, move from one minute to the next, live in the moment.

With each new day, God will reveal His power within you. He will lead you forward.

"Give thanks to the Lord, for He is good, for His loving-kindness lasts forever" (Psalm 136:1 NLV).

The Last Word

Springtime is when all Christians unite to celebrate Resurrection Sunday.

The sun was coming up on the first day of the week.
Mary Magdalene and the other Mary came to see [Jesus']
grave. At once the earth shook and an angel of the Lord came
down from heaven. He came and pushed back the stone from the
door and sat on it. His face was bright like lightning. His clothes
were white as snow.... The angel said to the women, "Do not be
afraid. I know you are looking for Jesus Who was nailed to the
cross. He is not here! He has risen from the dead as He said
He would. Come and see the place where the Lord lay.
Run fast and tell His followers that He is risen from
the dead." (Matthew 28:1–3, 5–7 NLV)

On this day, God gave us the best reason to be grateful. He raised Jesus from the grave to start His exalted life as Christ our Lord. His resurrection is our promise of eternal life if we choose to accept Him as our Savior.

Christ's resurrection restored what was lost, our perfect relationship with God. Every day, it wipes away sin and gives us hope not only for all the days of our lives but for eternity!

Thank God for Jesus. Thank Him for the gift of eternal life.

Week 4: DAY THREE
SUMMERTIME

Summertime is the season between the ages of about twenty through our midfifties, when we experience the most growth and ease into maturity. Springtime is over. The Bible says, "When the branch begins to grow and puts out its leaves, you know summer is near" (Mark 13:28 NLV).

Summer is the season when we dare to spread our wings and fly. Youth, freedom, all things light and lazy. We are open books with blank pages ready to fill. Now we are eager and willing to reach out and grab what life has to offer. Summer is a time of adventure, learning, and building careers, a season when days are longer and nights are warm and welcoming. So many new experiences. So much more to be thankful for.

This season offers some of the best parts of life. It is, perhaps, the most exciting time. But summer also brings storms. Whereas in spring we enjoyed the gentle rains that gave us puddles to splash in, summer storms arrive vicious and cruel, holding life lessons that make us afraid but also strengthen us and shape us into mature adults.

Imagine Jesus nearing the end of a busy summer day. He had just delivered the Sermon on the Mount. A huge crowd followed Him from the mountain and into Capernaum, where He healed the sick. Throughout the evening, Jesus cast out demons and continued making people well. As evening turned to night, He got into a boat with His disciples, and they sailed onto the Sea of Galilee. Jesus, tired from a long day's work, fell asleep.

At once a bad storm came over the [sea]. The waves were
covering the boat. Jesus was sleeping. His followers went to Him
and called, "Help us, Lord, or we will die!" [Jesus] said to them,
"Why are you afraid? You have so little faith!" Then He stood up.
He spoke sharp words to the wind and the waves. Then the wind
stopped blowing. [The] men were surprised and wondered about
it. They said, "What kind of a man is He? Even the winds
and the waves obey Him." (Matthew 8:24–27 NLV)

A summer storm can be a blessing in disguise. Just when we are afraid we might die, there is Jesus calming the waves and stopping the wind from blowing. Summertime is the season when our relationship with Him grows stronger. The storms teach us to trust Him and rest in His love. They help us appreciate even more the lazy, light summer days.

Maybe you are experiencing a light summer day right now, a time filled with sunshine and laughter. Or maybe you are caught in a summer storm and afraid. Thank God for the good days. Thank Him too for the storms that keep you spiritually alert. Thank Him for teaching you to pray and to trust and to grow. Thank God for this season of life and learning.

Thank God for summer days.

Unto thee, O God, do we give thanks, unto thee do we give thanks:
for that thy name is near thy wondrous works declare.

PSALM 75:1

The Blank Page

Maybe you are in your summer season right now, or maybe you have passed through it and are into a new season. Thinking about the summer season of life, make a list of your best achievements. Consider things you did outside your comfort zone, your spiritual growth, ways in which you matured, new things you learned, goals you reached. Once you've brainstormed your accomplishments, write a prayer to God. Thank Him specifically for each item on your list. Praise Him for the times you felt Him guiding you. Recognize the little miracles He did (the Godwinks) that led you to take unexpected paths or enter important relationships.

After you've written your prayer, tuck it away inside your Bible. On days when you feel discouraged, reread the prayer to remind you of all the great things God has done in your life. Then believe that the best is yet to come.

"I give thanks and praise to You, O God of my fathers. For You have given me wisdom and power" (Daniel 2:23 NLV).

⸙ The Last Word ⸙

Mythology is rife with stories of creatures and false gods. Daedalus, in Greek mythology, was an architect who built a giant maze under the court of King Minos.

A creature lived inside the maze: Minotaur, which was half man, half bull. King Minos wanted to keep Minotaur happy, so he locked Theseus, a prince, inside the maze as a human sacrifice for the creature. Trouble arrived when the king's daughter fell in love with Theseus. She persuaded Daedalus to reveal the way out of the maze, and discovering this, the angry king locked Daedalus and his son, Icarus, in a tower above his palace.

Daedalus created a means of escape: two sets of wings for himself and Icarus, wings made of feathers held together with wax. Daedalus taught his son to fly and warned him not to fly too high or the wings would melt. But Icarus didn't heed his father's warning. He flew too close to the sun, and the wings dissolved, sending him plummeting into the sea.

Fiction, of course, but it holds a lesson. Listen to your Father!

In the summer of our lives, we might forget God's teaching and soar too high with pride for our accomplishments. A lack of humility can send us tumbling down. Be grateful to God for teaching you to fly, but remember your achievements are thanks to Him. Instead of soaring high on wings made of wax, give God the glory. Someday, He will reward you with heavenly wings of gold.

Week 4: DAY FOUR
AUTUMN

Autumn is the season of life when we're ready to let go of summer's wild rhythm—the rushing to and from everywhere, raising children, advancing in our jobs, maintaining households, building relationships. We're ready to be done with the stress that comes at work, home, and other areas of our lives. Autumn tells us, "It's time to relax." Our children are old enough to marry now and give us grandchildren; our careers are winding down; we've grown in wisdom and learned what's really important in our lives. You might say it's time to reap what we have sown. We are like the farmer whose crops are brought in, and now he sits on a frosty autumn night in front of the fireplace enjoying a hot drink and a good book.

Yes, autumn is time to slow down and relax, but we still have a lot of living to do! Autumn is when we can reinvent ourselves. We have new freedom to choose what we want to do and where we want to live. Autumn is time to revisit the old hobbies and interests we set aside during the busy summer season. Family, friends, travel, and learning continue to be important; now we have more time to enjoy them. After retirement, we also have more time to give of ourselves and to pay forward some of the blessings God has granted us.

Volunteering is one way to stay active and engaged. According to the Bureau of Labor Statistics, people ages fifty-five and older make up more than 35 percent of those who volunteer. Think about all the wisdom you've gained in your life. It's time to share it. You can do so simply by being with young people and teaching them about living. Youth groups in your church, schools, and community are there for you to volunteer and pass along some of what you've learned. You can use your skills to help people in need; volunteer to build and renovate houses; cook and deliver meals to the sick, homeless, and elderly; teach others to read or speak a new language. You can help elect a candidate, take part in a fundraiser, work in a nonprofit thrift shop. So many possibilities to give back some of what God has given you.

Dr. Martin Luther King Jr. said, "Everybody can be great because everybody can serve. You don't have to have a college degree to serve. . . . You don't have to know about Plato and Aristotle to serve. You don't have to know Einstein's theory of relativity to serve. . . . You only need a heart full of grace, a soul generated by love. And you can be that servant."[22]

In the autumn season of life and in any life season, you can find ways to serve God. Service is one more way you can show God that you're grateful for all He's done for you.

Unto thee, O God, do we give thanks, unto thee do we give thanks:
for that thy name is near thy wondrous works declare.

PSALM 75:1

22   Martin Luther King Jr., "'The Drum Major Instinct,' Sermon Delivered at Ebenezer Baptist Church," Stanford: The Martin Luther King, Jr. Research and Education Institute, https://kinginstitute.stanford.edu/king-papers/documents/drum-major-instinct-sermon-delivered-ebenezer-baptist-church.

❧ The Blank Page ❦

As you pass through life's seasons, God plants seeds within you that grow into specific skills and talents. Make time today to think about and be grateful for the gifts He has given you. Then ask God how He wants you to share them with others.

* *What can you do to help children and teens in the springtime of their lives? How can you use what you have learned to lead them to transition more smoothly into summertime?*

* *In the summer season of life, how can you sharpen your God-given abilities? Summertime is the best time to plan how you might use some of your gifts to help yourself and others in your autumn and winter seasons.*

* *What are your plans for the autumn and winter seasons of life? If you are already there, what are you doing to serve God? Are you paying forward His gifts?*

Be willing to go where God leads you. Then step out courageously in faith ready to serve Him by serving others.

Each of you should use whatever gift you have received to serve others, as faithful stewards of God's grace in its various forms. If anyone speaks, they should do so as one who speaks the very words of God. If anyone serves, they should do so with the strength God provides, so that in all things God may be praised through Jesus Christ. To him be the glory and the power for ever and ever. Amen. (1 Peter 4:10–11 NIV)

❧ The Last Word ❧

*"Unto thee, O God, do we give thanks, unto thee
do we give thanks: for that thy name is near
thy wondrous works declare"* (Psalm 75:1).

Here are some additional ways to memorize this week's verse—
make it a family affair!

* *Create a cute little card with the verse written on it. Pack it in your spouse's or child's lunch bag.*

* *Make it a game. After family members have done their best to memorize the verse, one family member hides the scripture memory card. That person chooses another family member to find it, but before he or she begins looking for it, that person has to recite the verse from memory. Young children really enjoy this game!*

* *Make it a competition. If every family member can recite the verse from memory at dinnertime, provide a special after-dinner activity or treat.*

* *Be creative. See if your family can come up with some other games or challenges for memorizing scripture.*

Week 4: DAY FIVE
WINTER

Have we not all, amid life's petty strife,
Some pure ideal of a noble life
That once seemed possible? Did we not hear
The flutter of its wings, and feel it near,
And just within our reach? It was. And yet
We lost it in this daily. . .fret,
And now live idle in a vague regret.
But still our place is kept, and it will wait,
Ready for us to fill it, soon or late.
No star is ever lost we once have seen,
We always may be what we might have been.[23]

Those are Adelaide Anne Procter's words in her poem "A Legend of Provence." She reminds us that in our winter season, it's not too late to follow a dream.

All around us there are examples of late bloomers—people finding success in the winter years of life. The next time you pass that fast-food chicken restaurant, the one with the smiling colonel on its sign, remember that Harlan Sanders started his company when he was in his midsixties. Ten years later, he sold it for two million dollars, and then he remained active as its brand ambassador. Laura Ingalls Wilder is another example of someone who didn't allow age to get in her way. She published her first Little House book when she was sixty-five. She kept adding to the series and wrote the last book when she was seventy-six. She continued

---

23 Adelaide Procter, "Adelaide Anne Procter Verse: A Legend of Provence Poem," Classic Literature, https://classic-literature.co.uk/adelaide-anne-procter-verse-a-legend-of-provence-poem/.

to live on her farm and enjoyed communicating with her editors and fans until she died at age ninety.

God doesn't expect us to get old and give up! He wants us to keep going and squeeze every drop out of life. The Bible says, "Planted in the house of the Lord, they will grow well in the home of our God. They will still give fruit when they are old. They will be full of life and strength. And they will show that the Lord is faithful" (Psalm 92:13–15 NLV). God Himself says in Isaiah 46:4 (ESV), "Even to your old age I am he, and to gray hairs I will carry you." And Proverbs 16:31 (ESV) reminds us, "Gray hair is a crown of glory; it is gained in a righteous life."

Most late bloomers don't gain fame, but they find contentment living life fully. All around us, there are many Christians in their seventies and older who serve God and show their gratefulness to Him by continuing to do His work. Maybe you are one of them. Ernest Hemingway wrote in *The Old Man and the Sea*, "Now is no time to think of what you do not have. Think of what you can do with what there is." What great advice for the winter season of our lives!

Read again the last words of Adelaide Anne Procter's poem. Carry them with you to your winter season:

> *No star is ever lost we once have seen,*
> *We always may be what we might have been.*

Unto thee, O God, do we give thanks, unto thee do we give thanks:
for that thy name is near thy wondrous works declare.

PSALM 75:1

❧ The Blank Page ❧

Here is an activity you can do with your family or friends. Challenge yourself and others to complete a season of gratitude.

* *Decide on a specific length of time for your challenge.*

* *Begin each day of the challenge asking God to provide you with a grateful heart:*

  > "Dear God, I confess that I am not always mindful of the wonderful ways You work in my life and in the world around me. Today, make me keenly aware of Your presence. Open my eyes to Your blessings and give me a grateful heart. Amen."

* *Ask God to provide you with a theme for each day—one specific thing to examine with gratefulness. Themes could be people: individual family members, friends, coworkers; places: your workplace, for example; activities: things you do for fun, etc.*

* *At the end of every day, recite to God what you are grateful for. If you had trouble being thankful, tell God about that too, and ask Him to help you.*

* *Note what God is teaching you about gratefulness.*

* *At the end of your challenge, get together with the others in your group and share what you've learned.*

❧ *The Last Word* ❧

We can't end our exploration of the four seasons without visiting the words of King Solomon in the book of Ecclesiastes:

> *Everything on earth has its own time and its own season.*
> *There is a time for birth and death, planting and reaping,*
> *for killing and healing, destroying and building, for crying*
> *and laughing, weeping and dancing, for throwing stones and*
> *gathering stones, embracing and parting. There is a time*
> *for finding and losing, keeping and giving, for tearing*
> *and sewing, listening and speaking. There is also*
> *a time for love and hate, for war and peace.*
>
> *What do we gain by all of our hard work? I have seen what*
> *difficult things God demands of us. God makes everything*
> *happen at the right time. Yet none of us can ever fully*
> *understand all he has done, and he puts questions in our*
> *minds about the past and the future. I know the best thing we*
> *can do is to always enjoy life.* (Ecclesiastes 3:1–12 CEV)

Whatever season you are in right now, enjoy it! Be grateful to God because He is in control; He is with you and guiding you each day of your life.

Week 4: DAY SIX
GRATITUDE AND GRACE

None of us is perfect. We've displeased God and are undeserving of His loving-kindness (Romans 3:23). We make mistakes in every season of our lives. Our mistakes shape us, and how we react to them defines our character.

Some of us carry past mistakes into the present. We continuously beat ourselves up and decide we don't deserve anything good because we did something unforgivable. That isn't how God wants us to live. There is nothing He won't forgive us for. He loves us so much that He sent Jesus to pay the price for our sins. God gives us His grace unconditionally. He showers it on us at our lowest point, even when we know He isn't pleased by our behavior. Grace is His most precious gift—He shows His loving-kindness and favor to us even when we don't deserve it. Grace isn't about us doing something to please God, and it isn't about God being pleased with us. It is only about His beautiful unconditional love. At our worst, God wants us to remember that He loves us.

Children, in the spring of their lives, make mistakes all the time. Can you imagine as a parent if you never forgave your children for their mistakes? Would you kick them out of the house and never have anything to do with them? Of course not! You've made mistakes too. You understand. You have unconditional love for your children. That is the way God behaves toward you when you make mistakes. In all the seasons of your life, you are still His child and He loves you. Jesus says in Matthew 7:11 (NLV), "You are bad and you know how to give good things to your children. How much more will your

Father in heaven give good things to those who ask Him?"

We can go with complete trust to the throne of God with confidence that we will receive His loving-kindness and have His loving favor to help us whenever we need it (Hebrews 4:16). We can come to Him in our brokenness and sin, and His grace will lift us up in love.

Paul says in 1 Corinthians 15:10 (NIV), "But by the grace of God I am what I am, and his grace to me was not without effect. No, I worked harder than all of them—yet not I, but the grace of God that was with me." God's grace toward us results in our gratitude. It makes us want to work even harder to do what is right and please Him. His grace empowers us.

This week's memory verse reminds us to give thanks to God and acknowledge His wondrous works. God's grace *is* His most wonderful work. It is the heart of His love for us and His forgiveness.

If you are punishing yourself for past mistakes, forgive yourself and accept God's grace with gratitude. He loves you right now just as He has through all the seasons of your life.

Unto thee, O God, do we give thanks, unto thee do we give thanks:
for that thy name is near thy wondrous works declare.

PSALM 75:1

The Blank Page

Get in the habit of recognizing God's grace every day. At the end of each day, jot down the ways in which God showed you His kindness and mercy. When your family is together at the dinner table, encourage each person to share at least one observation of God's grace that day. Do this every day, and you will learn to live in grace and gratitude.

When you mess up, don't run away from God. Go find Him! Tell Him you are sorry, thank Him for extending His grace to you, and let that be enough. Learn from your mistakes and then leave them alone.

To everything there is a season, and in each season, we do things we regret. When you pass through a dark season, when you lose your way and behave in ways that aren't pleasing to God, don't make the mistake of not recognizing that His grace is there waiting for you to accept it. He wants you to have it—and it's free. Choose grace! Allow it to overpower your past transgressions and create in you a new beginning.

If you are struggling today with accepting the gift of God's grace, here is another Bible verse you should commit to memory. Recite it to yourself often and believe it:

"All of us have sinned and fallen short of God's glory. But God treats us much better than we deserve, and because of Christ Jesus, he freely accepts us and sets us free from our sins" (Romans 3:23–24 CEV).

❧ The Last Word ❧

In the spring and summer seasons of life, John Newton was known as "the great blasphemer." He rejected God and even tried to rob others of their belief in Him. Then, one summer day, John was aboard a ship when a great storm hit. As water washed over the deck and swallowed some of his shipmates, John worked furiously pumping water trying to keep the ship afloat. "God have mercy!" he shouted. He continued praying, taking the helm steering the ship. After many hours, the winds died down and the battered ship drifted to an island. John Newton's life had been ever changed by God's grace—and John was grateful. He accepted God's loving-kindness and turned his life over to Him.

Years later, in the autumn of life, John recalled the grace God extended to him in the storm and in all the storms he'd weathered since. He was in the ministry by then, preaching the Gospel of Christ and composing hymns for his Sunday evening services. Remembering God's grace that day when he was caught in a raging sea, John Newton penned the words to what would become one of the most well-known hymns in history, "Amazing Grace."

> *...Through many dangers, toils, and snares,*
> *I have already come;*
> *'Tis grace hath brought me safe thus far,*
> *And grace will lead me home.*
> *The Lord has promised good to me,*
> *His Word my hope secures;*
> *He will my Shield and Portion be,*
> *As long as life endures.*

Week 4: DAY SEVEN
PUTTING IT ALL TOGETHER

When we set out on new adventures in life, as one season dissolves into the next, we know God is always with us. He awakens us, leads and guides us, and at the end of the day, He is there to tuck us into our beds. He forms us in our mothers' wombs and births us into the springtime of life. He opens our eyes to all things new and sets in our hearts the wonder of His creations. He leads us into our summer months, where He refines and sharpens us, building our characters and guiding us into maturity. We grow in our love for Him. We recognize with gratitude the many things He has done for us and continues to do. In autumn, a season of giving back, we reach out to those in every season of life and help them weather their storms. Even in winter, God is with us, whispering in our ears, "It's never too late to try something new." Our seasons change, but God does not. He remains constant throughout all the seasons of life. This is what the Bible says:

* *"Have you not known? Have you not heard? The God Who lives forever is the Lord, the One Who made the ends of the earth. He will not become weak or tired. His understanding is too great for us to begin to know"* (Isaiah 40:28 NLV).

* *"Whatever is good and perfect comes to us from God. He is the One Who made all light. He does not change. No shadow is made by His turning"* (James 1:17 NLV).

* *"God does not change His mind when He chooses men and gives them His gifts"* (Romans 11:29 NLV).

God is the One we can always cling to. He is our root, our anchor. There are no storms in life He can't lead us through. Praise God and give Him thanks for being the One you can count on.

Thank Him too for His amazing grace. Throughout our lives, when we trip and fall, God is there to pick us up, clean us off, patch our hurts, and tell us to "carry on." When we behave in ways that displease Him, God is ready to forgive us and help us to learn from our mistakes. His grace rains down on us. It is deep and wide like the ocean. It calls us into a relationship of love.

In each life season, if we make God the center of our being, we will discover new reasons to thank Him. He showers us with blessings, answers our prayers, provides for our needs, protects us, loves us, and forgives us. He keeps our bodies working, and even when our bodies come to the end, He provides us with the greatest gift of all—the gift of eternal life, being with Him forever in heaven.

Give thanks to God for the seasons of your life. "Give thanks to the God of heaven, for His loving-kindness lasts forever" (Psalm 136:26 NLV).

Unto thee, O God, do we give thanks, unto thee do we give thanks:
for that thy name is near thy wondrous works declare.

PSALM 75:1

❧ The Blank Page ❧

As you've read the devotions in this book, you've noticed even more Bible verses than those on the Bible memory cards. Maybe some of them have made an impression on you. Write them on your heart!

Second Timothy 3:16–17 (NIV) says, "All Scripture is God-breathed and is useful for teaching, rebuking, correcting and training in righteousness, so that the servant of God may be thoroughly equipped for every good work." Memorizing scripture is the most important tool you have in every season of life. It helps you prepare, set priorities, and build courage. It readies you for whatever you encounter in life whether it is to lead, follow, get along with others, or handle a crisis.

Scripture is inspired by God and always true. Like Him, it doesn't change. The Bible is there to guide you. It is your handbook, equipping you to serve the Lord in all that you do. The Bible is one key way that God communicates with you, leading you through life and in your life's work.

Memorizing a scripture verse is not something you do just once. To keep from forgetting your memory verses, review them often by reading them in your Bible. Memorize again any part you memorized incorrectly or have forgotten.

Let's review this week's verse: "Unto thee, O God, do we give thanks, unto thee do we give thanks: for that thy name is near thy wondrous works declare" (Psalm 75:1).

The Last Word

Father God, I thank You for being near to me through every season of my life, for leading me and guiding my every step. I am so grateful for the adventures and celebrations, the lessons You've taught me, and the ways You have shaped me to be the person I am today. I praise You for Your wondrous deeds. Every day I recognize new blessings and reasons to be thankful. I am especially grateful that You forgive my sins and offer me grace unconditionally. Your love fills my heart with gratitude. May I honor You through everything I do all the days of my life. Amen.

Week 5

GRATEFUL FOR GOD, OUR HEAVENLY POTTER

O come, let us worship and bow down:
let us kneel before the LORD our maker.
For he is our God; and we are
the people of his pasture,
and the sheep of his hand.

PSALM 95:6–7

Week 5: DAY ONE
GOD OUR MAKER

Psalm 95:6–7, this week's memory verse, reminds us to thank God for creating us, not only for making our bodies but also for molding us into people who can enjoy life fully and meet its challenges with faith. The Bible tells us that God is the potter and we are the clay (Isaiah 64:8). He artfully shapes our character and refines those traits that are pleasing to Him. Working within us, He shepherds our hearts, leading us to be more like Jesus.

This week, we'll look at some of the character traits built on our relationship and commitment to God. It's important to remember that character traits are different than feelings. Our feelings come and go, changing like the wind, but traits are steadfast. Good traits are gifts from God that help us navigate through life, relate to others, and grow in our relationships. God is constantly enhancing and refining them, shaping us to be better each day. The Bible lists some of these traits in Galatians 5:22–23 (NIV)—"love, joy, peace, forbearance, kindness, goodness, faithfulness, gentleness and self-control"—but there are many others: dependability, resourcefulness, sincerity, and tolerance, for example.

When you welcome God into your heart, He begins working on your soul. His work is never-ending. There's always room for improvement! Philippians 1:6 (NLV) says, "God Who began the good work in you will keep on working in you until the day Jesus Christ comes again." Unlike human artists who create one work of art and then move to the next, God is working on you all the days of your life. He never says, "I'm done with you," and then goes on to someone else. God's goal is to make you the best you can be while you live here on earth. His masterpiece—you—won't be perfect and complete until that glorious day when you enter heaven and meet your Maker face-to-face.

It's not always easy to endure God's character building. He allows us to face trials in our lives, and how we learn to respond to them builds our character. Paul says in Romans 5:3 (NLV), "We are glad for our troubles also. We know that troubles help us learn not to give up." When facing challenges, God builds our hope, strength, courage, and resilience. You might think of it as somewhat like remodeling a house. You tear off a roof and replace it with a better one, or you rip out the cabinets and counters in your outdated kitchen and bring in everything new. For a while, during the remodeling process, it's a mess. But the end result is worth it.

When we study the Bible and especially Jesus, we become more aware of the character traits God wants us to have. As we see ourselves growing, changing, and becoming better people, it's time to get on our knees, like this week's verse says, and worship God, giving thanks to Him for shaping us in Christ's image and equipping us for life.

O come, let us worship and bow down: let us kneel before the LORD our maker. For he is our God; and we are the people of his pasture, and the sheep of his hand.

PSALM 95:6–7

✿ The Blank Page ✿

Begin this week by doing some soul searching.

- *Think about your best character traits—those good behaviors you exhibit all the time because they are a part of you; things like patience, punctuality, and kindness. Write them down.*

- *Next, make a list of traits you don't have or those that need building. Maybe you lack confidence, are often nervous and afraid, wish you were more attentive to the needs of your family and others, tend to procrastinate, or lack motivation.*

- *Focus on one specific trait you'd like to improve. Pray and ask God to build up that trait within you. Then begin to act on improving it. This should be an ongoing activity. As you become comfortable with a new or improved trait, add another.*

- *Recognize the ways God is working in your heart to build your character, and honor Him by giving Him thanks.*

Here's something to think about:

"The expression of Christian character is not good doing, but God-likeness. If the Spirit of God has transformed you within, you will exhibit Divine characteristics in your life, not good human characteristics. God's life in us expresses itself as God's life, not as human life trying to be godly."[24] *—Oswald Chambers*

---

24   Oswald Chambers, *My Utmost for His Highest Classic Edition* (Uhrichsville, OH: Barbour Publishing, 2014), 10.

The Last Word

Sometimes, a scripture verse paints a picture in our minds. The Twenty-Third Psalm, "The Lord is my shepherd," is a scripture passage most of us know and can recite from memory. We can imagine the Lord as a caring shepherd leading us to where pastures are green and the water is still and cool. We can see Him calming and comforting us when we are afraid, protecting us from danger, and providing for all our needs.

This week's memory verse is another that paints a word picture: "O come, let us worship and bow down: let us kneel before the LORD our maker. For he is our God; and we are the people of his pasture, and the sheep of his hand" (Psalm 95:6–7).

As you work to memorize it, visualize the picture it paints: you, bowing before God, kneeling and worshipping Him for making you the best you can be. Envision Him as your loving, caring shepherd.

Memorizing scripture can be easier when you imagine yourself inside God's Word, experiencing what He has to offer you.

LOVE

"I love you." Words we say as we head out the door in the morning. Words we say when ending a phone call: "Love you. Bye." Words that slip casually into our vocabularies. They are important words though. We need to hear them so we feel loved.

But love is much more than a feeling. Paul lists some of its characteristics: "Love is kind and patient, never jealous, boastful, proud, or rude. Love isn't selfish or quick tempered. It doesn't keep a record of wrongs that others do. Love rejoices in the truth, but not in evil. Love is always supportive, loyal, hopeful, and trusting" (1 Corinthians 13:4–7 CEV). In other words, love is a combination of character traits working together. Paul says if he could speak all the world's languages and even the language of angels, if he could understand all of life's secrets, he would be nothing unless he loved others. The greatest of all good character traits, Paul says, is love (1 Corinthians 13:1–2, 13 CEV).

You've heard the phrase "love at first sight." Well, God loved you even before He saw you. The idea of you and how great you could be was in His mind before He gave you a human form. God made you—all of us—in His image (Genesis 1:27). The Bible says, "God is love" (1 John 4:8). Everything about Him characterizes what love is, and He made us to model ourselves on His love. True love takes work. It requires that we love others with commitment, patience, forgiveness, diligence, truthfulness, and availability—the way God loves us.

God made us to be loving human beings. John says in 1 John

4:7–8 (NLV), "Love comes from God. Those who love are God's children and they know God. Those who do not love do not know God because God is love." There is no true love when we live apart from God. Striving to love others the way He loves us is what brings us nearest to Him.

When others show their love for us, it feels good. But when God shows His love for us, it *is* good! Everything God does He does for us out of love. That by itself is reason to be grateful to Him, but think for a moment about the sacrifice He made so your heart could be joined forever with His in love: "For God so loved the world that He gave His only Son. Whoever puts his trust in God's Son will not be lost but will have life that lasts forever" (John 3:16 NLV). And it's not just your life that will last forever, but God's love that will be with you forever.

Worship God. Thank Him for His love and also the love you share with others. Then work hard to build up all those traits that lead you toward loving others the way that God loves you.

O come, let us worship and bow down: let us kneel before the Lord our maker. For he is our God; and we are the people of his pasture, and the sheep of his hand.

PSALM 95:6–7

🌿 The Blank Page 🌿

Today's activity will get you thinking about godly character traits. There are three parts to this exercise.

1. Using the letters in the words *GOD'S LOVE*, list one godly trait for each letter. (A godly character trait is one that, when put into practice, honors God.) Two are already completed for you:

G

O Obedience

D

S

L

O

V Versatility

E

2. List five more positive traits that you believe are pleasing to God.

3. Complete this sentence: I am most grateful to God for these character traits He has put in my heart: _____, _____, and _____.

❧ The Last Word ❧

Read and meditate on these quotes about love.

"Learning to love unselfishly is not an easy task. It runs counter to our self-centered nature."[25] —Rick Warren

"In biblical thinking, genuine love exists only when good works are done in a context where God rather than the doer gets the credit."[26] —Daniel Fuller

"In the New Testament, love is more of a verb than a noun. It has more to do with acting than with feeling. The call to love is not so much a call to a certain state of feeling as it is to a quality of action."[27] —R. C. Sproul

"What does love look like? It has the hands to help others. It has the feet to hasten to the poor and needy. It has eyes to see misery and want. It has the ears to hear the sighs and sorrows of men. That is what love looks like." —Augustine

"We have come to know and believe the love God has for us. God is love. If you live in love, you live by the help of God and God lives in you." —1 John 4:16 NLV

"Where Love is, God is." —Leo Tolstoy

"I pray that you will be able to understand how wide and how long and how high and how deep His love is." —Ephesians 3:18 NLV

---

25   Rick Warren, *The Purpose Driven Life: What on Earth Am I Here For?* (Grand Rapids, MI: Zondervan, 2018), Day 16.

26   Daniel Fuller, *The Unity of the Bible: Unfolding God's Plan for Humanity* (Grand Rapids, MI: Zondervan, 1992).

27   R. C. Sproul, *Essential Truths of the Christian Faith* (Carol Stream, IL: Tyndale House, 2011), 257.

DETERMiNATiON

The word *determined* means having made a firm decision and being resolved not to change it. How determined are you? When you set a goal, how willing are you to reach it?

It's important to recognize the difference between the positive character trait determination and its negative counterpart stubbornness. One is self-willed; the other is willing. If you're stubborn, you won't give up even if you hear God's voice saying, "Stop!" It's your will against His. Determination is your willingness to keep moving forward when God says, "Yes!" It's you saying to God, "I will follow You no matter what!"

The Bible is filled with stories about determination. Ruth was determined to stay with Naomi (Ruth 1:18). Daniel was determined to stay true to God instead of worshipping a king (Daniel 6). First Chronicles 12 tells about a huge army fighting with determination to help David become king of Israel (v. 38). And when David was king, he was determined to find God even when God seemed far away. He prayed, "I have looked for You with all my heart" (Psalm 119:10 NLV).

In the Gospels, many were determined to find Jesus, believing He would heal them. One of the best determination stories is in Mark 2. Jesus was teaching inside a crowded room. The Bible says there was standing room only, and the crowd spilled outside blocking the door. Four men came carrying a disabled friend on a mat. When they couldn't get through the crowd to Jesus, they were determined to find a way inside. They wanted their friend healed, so they cut a hole in the roof above Jesus and lowered the man down. "When Jesus saw how much faith they had, he said to the [disabled] man, 'My friend, your sins are forgiven'.... 'Get up! Pick up your mat and go on home.' The man got right up. He picked up his mat and went out while everyone watched in amazement. They praised God and said, 'We have never seen anything like this!' " (Mark 2:5, 11–12 CEV). The friends' determination resulted in something good.

When we seek God with determination, we can be grateful to always find Him. He says, "You will call upon Me and come and pray to Me, and I will listen to you. You will look for Me and find Me, when you look for Me with all your heart" (Jeremiah 29:12–13 NLV).

Determination gets bigger when it's rooted in God. When you seek Him with all your heart, your relationship with Him grows in faith and trust. God builds up that determined character trait within you and guides you to use it in other areas of your life.

Do you sense God leading you toward a specific goal? Pray and ask Him to get you there. Be like those friends in Mark 2. Find a way around the obstacles. Don't give up. Remember to be grateful, and thank God for guiding you each step along the way.

O come, let us worship and bow down: let us kneel before the
LORD our maker. For he is our God; and we are the people
of his pasture, and the sheep of his hand.
PSALM 95:6–7

The Blank Page

There is a quotation attributed to Saint Ignatius of Loyola: "Pray as if God will take care of all; act as if all is up to you." People with a strong sense of determination make plans that keep them moving toward their goals.

Here is a ten-step plan you can put into action when there's something you hope to accomplish.

1. Set a goal. Be as specific as you can.
2. Plan manageable steps leading to the goal.
3. Pray and ask God to help you set realistic deadlines.
4. Make a plan to overcome any negative thinking or obstacles that get in your way.
5. Write down five encouraging Bible verses you can turn to for support.
6. Rely on your God-given skills and talents to encourage you as you move forward.
7. When in doubt, ask God to give your confidence a boost.
8. If faced with a difficult decision, seek God's will.
9. Take breaks when necessary.
10. Thank God for His help.

"O Lord my God, I will give thanks to You with all my heart. I will bring honor to Your name forever" (Psalm 86:12 NLV).

Think about this:

What are the benefits of determination?

Determination is a character trait that not only helps you achieve your goals but also helps God accomplish His goals through you!

The Last Word

When an obstacle gets in your way, find encouragement in these words from the poem "Can't" by Edgar A. Guest.

Can't is a word none should speak without blushing;
To utter it should be a symbol of shame;
Ambition and courage it daily is crushing;
It blights a man's purpose and shortens his aim.
Despise it with all of your hatred of error;
Refuse it the lodgment it seeks in your brain;
Arm against it as a creature of terror,
And all that you dream of you some day shall gain.

Can't is the word that is foe to ambition,
An enemy ambushed to shatter your will;
Its prey is forever the man with a mission
And bows but to courage and patience and skill.
Hate it, with hatred that's deep and undying,
For once it is welcomed 'twill break any man;
Whatever the goal you are seeking, keep trying
And answer this demon by saying: "I can." [28]

Thank God for His power working through you, helping you to reach your goal.

Remember this Bible verse and write it on your heart: "With God all things are possible" (Matthew 19:26 NIV).

---

28   Edgar A. Guest, *A Heap O' Livin'* (Chicago: Reilly & Britton Company, 1916). Retrieved from http://www.gutenberg.org/cache/epub/328/pg328-images.html.

Week 5: DAY FOUR
COMPASSION

"The LORD, the LORD, the compassionate and gracious God, slow to anger, abounding in love and faithfulness" (Exodus 34:6 NIV). Oh, how grateful we should be to God for His compassion!

Webster's dictionary defines *compassion* as "a sympathetic consciousness of others' distress together with a desire to alleviate it." God shows His compassion to us every day. He is aware of everything that happens in our lives, and when we suffer, He wants to relieve our distress. When suffering comes because of our own mistakes, God is forgiving, "gracious and compassionate, slow to anger and abounding in love" (Nehemiah 9:17 NIV).

Compassion is one of God's traits that is crucial for us to learn. If we learn compassion, then other good traits come with it: forgiveness, graciousness, patience, love, generosity, hospitality, justice, attentiveness, sincerity, tolerance. When we work hard to refine that one trait, compassion, we open our hearts to allow God to build a tower of good traits inside us.

Consciousness is the first step toward becoming more compassionate. In today's busy world, it's easy to miss people around us who could benefit from our compassion. The crabby coworker might be dealing with a crisis at home. The sullen teenager could be a victim of cyber-bullying. The sad-looking stranger who sits in the back of the church and doesn't speak to anyone might be all alone in the world. God wants us to open our eyes to all the ways we can reach out with compassion to others.

This week's memory card, Psalm 95:6–7, reminds us we are the people of God's pasture and the sheep of His hand. In a similar way, Mark 6:34 (NIV) says, "When Jesus. . .saw a large crowd, he had compassion on them, because they were like sheep without a shepherd. So he began teaching them many things." Our Shepherd is willing to teach us. If we ask Him to give us lessons on compassion, He surely will answer our prayer. He will open our eyes to how He might react to the crabby coworker, the sullen teen, and the sad-looking stranger. We can learn to be the tool He uses to alleviate someone's suffering.

To become more compassionate, practice being aware of the people around you. Get in the habit of entering into someone's suffering instead of running from it. Ask yourself and God what you can do to relieve someone's distress. It could be something as small as allowing the woman without a shopping cart, juggling an armload of groceries, to go ahead of you in the checkout line. Or, it could be something bigger, like taking a neighbor to his chemo appointments, sitting with him, and then making sure he is safely settled at home.

Thank God for His compassion toward you, but don't stop there. Compassion takes practice. Allow God to shape you into a more compassionate person, and ask Him how you can extend His compassion to others.

O come, let us worship and bow down: let us kneel before the
Lord our maker. For he is our God; and we are the people
of his pasture, and the sheep of his hand.
Psalm 95:6–7

The Blank Page

Look for people who are struggling. Look beyond your circle of family, friends, and acquaintances. Keep your eyes open for strangers in distress who might need a helping hand.

Practice compassion today. If you see a need, do your best to fill it. Try to see life from someone else's perspective. Exercise all those good traits you already possess. Be caring, humble, generous, and tolerant. Listen without judging. Be accepting, forgiving, loving, and kind. Respect others. Offer encouragement. Ask yourself if there is something you can do to help others achieve their goals.

One small act of compassion goes a long way. Open a door for someone. Offer to help carry groceries. Hug your friend. Take time to really listen to your kids and ask questions like "What do you need? How can I help?" If you see a coworker struggling to get her work done, offer to take an item off her to-do list. Even a little help is better than none, and it shows that you care.

There is another part to your assignment today. Identify one person in your life who needs compassion in a big way. Be the hands of Jesus, and help alleviate that person's suffering.

"People may excite in themselves a glow of compassion, not by toasting their feet at the fire, and saying: 'Lord, teach me compassion,' but by going and seeking an object that requires compassion." —Henry Ward Beecher

☘ *The Last Word* ☘

Memorizing a scripture verse can be easier if you think about its general message.

* *Ask other Christians how they interpret a specific verse and the ways they apply it to their lives.*

* *Do an online search to find commentaries for almost every verse in the Bible. Simply type in the scripture reference, for example Psalm 95:6–7, and the word* commentary *and you will discover links to sites where you can read what others have said.*

* *You can also read sermons online based on specific Bible verses. To find them, type in a scripture reference followed by the word* sermon *and you'll be led to pastors' sermons based on that scripture.*

When you delve into the meaning of a verse, you will not only remember its words, but you will also apply its message to your personal situations. Try it with this week's verse: "O come, let us worship and bow down: let us kneel before the LORD our maker. For he is our God; and we are the people of his pasture, and the sheep of his hand" (Psalm 95:6–7).

Week 5: DAY FIVE
STRENGTH AND COURAGE

When you hear the word *strong*, what do you think of? Maybe it calls up images of muscle-bound men like Samson in the Bible or Martins Licis, winner of the 2019 World's Strongest Man Competition. Or maybe the word turns your thoughts to powerful women like Judge Deborah in the Bible or female political leaders like German chancellor Angela Merkel, who was chosen by *Forbes* as the world's most powerful woman in 2019.

When you hear the word *strong*, do you think of yourself? Strength is another good character trait that comes from God. It is linked to courage, and the two working together driven by God's power make it possible for you to overcome any obstacle that gets in your way.

Fear is strength's competitor. You can choose to fight it or run from it. God says you should fight: "Have I not told you? Be strong and have strength of heart! Do not be afraid or lose faith. For the Lord your God is with you anywhere you go" (Joshua 1:9 NLV). Whatever trouble you face, you can trust God to go through it with you and make His power available to you.

In 2018, Christian singer and songwriter Francesca Battistelli released "The Breakup Song." Battistelli said she wanted fear out of her life for good so she wrote the song as her anthem. The lyrics speak directly to fear. Its message is that fear doesn't own us. We are strong, brave, and free to choose courage. Fear isn't welcome in our lives! Her song soared into the top ten, and its official music video received more than thirteen million views. "The Breakup

Song" became the anthem for many others fighting fear, proof that you aren't alone in your struggle against it. The best way to overcome fear is to break up with it forever.

Be grateful to God for giving you everything you need for a successful breakup. The key to sending fear packing is to stop feeding it. Increase your faith in God, and trust Him to lead you into that beautiful character trait courage. Think about young David in the Bible. An army of supposedly brave soldiers was afraid of that one big warrior, Goliath. But David, with God's power backing him, stood fast and firm against Goliath and overpowered him with a slingshot and a single stone. You can do that too.

Choose courage today. Pray and thank God for being the One who carries your burdens. Tell Him you have faith in Him to lead you through whatever gets in your way. When fear stands tall, like a Goliath in your path, be strong. Hand your slingshot to God, and allow Him to take the first shot. Then get ready to become the powerful, courageous person He wants you to be.

"For God did not give us a spirit of fear. He gave us a spirit of power" (2 Timothy 1:7 NLV).

O come, let us worship and bow down: let us kneel before the LORD our maker. For he is our God; and we are the people of his pasture, and the sheep of his hand.
PSALM 95:6-7

❧ The Blank Page ❧

Gratitude is one way of dealing with fear. When something frightening gets in your way, you can say, "Thank You, God, because You are about to do something great through me to overcome this obstacle." When you see fear as an opportunity instead of your enemy, you open the door for God to teach you how to fight. Gratitude reminds you that you aren't fighting alone. You have a partner so big and strong, nothing can get in His way.

Make a list today of things you are afraid of. Then switch your thoughts to gratitude. For example, if you are afraid of getting sick, you can be grateful for people who will help you—doctors, nurses, friends, family. When that fear arises, pray: "God, I'm afraid of getting sick, but I'm grateful that You have a plan if that happens. You've already lined up all the help I'll need if I ever have to face that fear."

Do it for each item on your list. When you get in the habit of immediately striking fear with gratefulness, you will discover that fear and gratitude can't coexist. Gratitude will always win and give you power. Gratitude makes you strong. It might not change the situation in the moment, but it gives you strength to endure with assurance that you and God will get through it together.

The Last Word

"The Bowman and the Lion"
A fable by Aesop

A very skillful bowman went to the mountains in search of game, but all the beasts of the forest fled at his approach. The Lion alone challenged him to combat. The Bowman immediately shot out an arrow and said to the Lion: "I send thee my messenger, that from him thou mayest learn what I myself shall be when I assail thee." The wounded Lion rushed away in great fear, and when a Fox who had seen it all happen told him to be of good courage and not to back off at the first attack he replied: "You counsel me in vain; for if he sends so fearful a messenger, how shall I abide the attack of the man himself?"[29]

You are that bowman! When faced by a lion of an obstacle, you can send it rushing away in fear just by putting your faith in God and being willing to strike the first blow. When fear challenges you to combat, say to it, "God gives me power, and He will overcome you!" Then keep moving forward with faith.

---

29   Aesop, *Aesop's Fables*. Updated October 28, 2016. Retrieved from http://www.gutenberg .org/files/21/21-h/21-h.htm.

Week 5: DAY SIX
FORGIVENESS

"I forgive you." Those words offered with sincerity are enough to fill a heart with gratitude. When we've offended someone and are repentant, the words *I forgive you* are like music to our ears. They comfort and soothe us. We can finally rest and start to heal. Jesus says forgiveness is tied to the way we love. "The one who has been forgiven little, loves little" (Luke 7:47 NLV). Forgiveness allows us to love again.

Some people are born able to forgive without hesitation, but for most, forgiveness is a learned character trait. A forgiving person has come to recognize true repentance. She tries to understand the motive behind an offense, and she is aware of her own transgressions. She cares about her relationships. She is moved by the suffering of an offender. A person who has learned forgiveness understands that it's a choice: it is more difficult to forgive than it is to be forgiven—but we need to forgive.

Forgiving others frees our hearts from anger and bitterness. It allows God's love to bring about healing. Forgiveness does not mean that a relationship or trust has to be restored. Forgiveness is more about the heart. It means not allowing ourselves to continue to suffer for wrongs done to us. We can make a conscious choice to let go of an offense and leave the rest to God. Paul says it this way in Romans 12:19 (NLV): "Christian brothers, never pay back someone for the bad he has done to you. Let the anger of God take care of the other person. The Holy Writings say, 'I will pay back to them what they should get, says the Lord.' "

In God's eyes, sin is sin. We are as much in need of His for-giveness as those who offend us. Jesus says in Matthew 6:14–15 (NLV): "If you forgive people their sins, your Father in heaven will forgive your sins also. If you do not forgive people their sins, your Father will not forgive your sins." Think about that. We need to forgive so that we too can be forgiven.

Forgiveness requires gratefulness to our heavenly Father for the simple reason that He is ready to forgive us daily, minute by minute, for our sins. When we understand our need to be forgiven by Him, then it is easier for us to forgive others. The healing power of His forgiveness brings us nearer to Him. It sets inside us another character trait, humility. We come to understand that we are equal to others in our need for forgiveness.

If you need to forgive someone today, do it because God says it's the right thing to do. Or maybe you need someone to forgive *you*. Take it to God. Ask Him to change hearts and to bring healing into your situation. If you don't get the forgiveness you need, know that God loves you. Then leave it with Him. Let His forgiveness be enough.

O come, let us worship and bow down: let us kneel before the
LORD our maker. For he is our God; and we are the people
of his pasture, and the sheep of his hand.

PSALM 95:6-7

The Blank Page

Today, you have a writing assignment: Write to God expressing your gratitude for His forgiveness. You could write Him a letter, poem, or even a prayer. Be specific. Thank Him for forgiving you for those times when you did things you knew would not please Him, the times you were so focused on yourself that you forgot about Him, even times when you willingly shut Him out of your life.

First John 1:9 (NLV) says, "If we tell [God] our sins, He is faithful and we can depend on Him to forgive us of our sins. He will make our lives clean from all sin." *If* is the key word—*if* you tell God about your sins, He will forgive you. Don't skip this part of your assignment. If you would rather not write to God, speak to Him. Pray and ask Him to forgive you. Convey your gratitude to Him for His ongoing gift of forgiveness.

God's forgiveness is free and unconditional. He isn't like humans, counting up wrongs and remembering the transgressions of others. He says in Isaiah 43:25 (NCV), "I, I am the One who erases all your sins, for my sake; I will not remember your sins."

Accept God's gift of forgiveness today, then offer your forgiveness to others.

❧ The Last Word ❧

Forgiveness is a process. It requires that we forgive over and over the person who hurt us. Anger, bitterness, and pain cut deep. We might never completely heal the hurt, but we can lessen it by calling on God whenever those negative feelings surge inside us.

We can

* *surrender the right to get even by meditating on Paul's words in Romans 12:19 (NLV): "Christian brothers, never pay back someone for the bad he has done to you. Let the anger of God take care of the other person. The Holy Writings say, 'I will pay back to them what they should get, says the Lord.'"*

* *stop being the victim. Yes, you were wronged, and it hurt. But dwelling on that thought keeps you imprisoned with all kinds of negative thoughts as your cell mates. Archbishop Desmond Tutu wrote in his book* No Future without Forgiveness, *"In the act of forgiveness we are declaring our faith in the future. . . . We are saying here is a chance to make a new beginning."*[30]

* *focus on the future. Each morning, ask God to lead you forward and help you leave what happened in the past. Each evening, end the day with gratitude.*

---

30   Desmond Tutu, *No Future without Forgiveness* (New York: Doubleday, 2000), 273.

Week 5: DAY SEVEN
PUTTING IT ALL TOGETHER

Anne Frank quoted her father in her diary: "All children must look after their own upbringing. Parents can only. . .put them on the right paths, but the final forming of a person's character lies in their own hands."[31] How true! At birth, our heavenly Father sets us on the right path. He puts in our hearts everything we need to build good character traits, but He leaves it to us to form our character to honor Him.

This week, you explored several good traits and how to enhance them. You learned that godly love means loving with commitment, patience, forgiveness, diligence, and truthfulness. You thought about the difference between determination and stubbornness. You recognized that determination helps you achieve your goals and also opens the door for God to accomplish His work through you. You became more aware of the people around you who needed compassion, and you discovered that practicing compassion builds up other good character traits like forgiveness, graciousness, patience, love, generosity, attentiveness, and tolerance. You thought about fighting fear and choosing courage, and you spent time pondering your need to forgive others. Throughout this week, you identified some of your strongest traits and discovered others that need work.

What about gratefulness? Is that a strong trait? Do you honor God by thanking Him all the time and in every situation? In Romans 1:21 (NLV), Paul says, "They did know God, but they did not

---

31   Anne Frank, *Anne Frank: The Diary of a Young Girl* (New York: Bantam, 1993), 260.

honor Him. . . . They were not thankful to Him and thought only of foolish things. Their foolish minds became dark." A mind set on traits that are not from God results in a dark heart, one that shuts out God and His good works.

Are you satisfied with your degree of gratefulness? There is always room for improvement. You can become even more grateful by learning to praise God for every little thing. Praise Him in the car, while walking your dog, when making meals. When your mind sinks into oblivion or a dark place, praise God for His goodness! Build up your gratitude through prayer. Talk with your heavenly Father all the time. Tell Him what troubles you. Thank Him for His willingness to help you and for always giving you His best. Become more grateful to Him for the silver linings. Remember that in every difficult challenge you can find something good. Maybe that something is building another positive trait. When you become more grateful, it leads to a transformed life, one more aligned with God and all His positive attributes. Gratefulness to Him increases your sense of contentment and peace.

Take a minute right now to thank God for setting you on the right path. Then promise yourself to work at becoming more grateful. As your gratefulness grows, God will change your perspective. When you begin to look at life through His eyes, you will be amazed by the beauty you see.

O come, let us worship and bow down: let us kneel before the
Lord our maker. For he is our God; and we are the people
of his pasture, and the sheep of his hand.

PSALM 95:6–7

❧ The Blank Page ❧

*"O come, let us worship and bow down: let us kneel before the
LORD our maker. For he is our God; and we are the people of
his pasture, and the sheep of his hand"* (Psalm 95:6–7).

Allow this week's memory verse to serve as a reminder that
God is more than your Maker. He is also the Shepherd of your
soul. He is the One who leads you to become the best you can be.

As you work to memorize the verse, think about self-awareness.
Track your negative feelings and emotions. Where do they come
from? Decide what's causing them. Act to get rid of each cause by
attacking it with a godly trait. Are you angry? Maybe you need to
work harder at compassion or forgiveness. Do you feel anxious?
Maybe you need to become more ambitious, determined, or patient. Self-awareness alerts you to those negative traits God wants
you to change.

Change requires hard work, but making positive changes to
your character opens the door for God to use those changes as
blessings. How willing are you to become the person you know
God wants you to be? How willing are you to change? Worship
and bow down to God. Kneel before the Lord your Maker and ask
Him to lead you.

The Last Word

Dear God, I need You. I bow before You today acknowledging You as my Creator. I come to You with a grateful heart, knowing that You are leading me and shaping me to become more like You. Make me aware of those negative character traits that displease You. Help me to become more caring, compassionate, and forgiving. Form me into a better person, someone who is kind, patient, and accessible; someone who will help others to reach their goals and fulfill their needs. Let the perfect light of Your love shine through me. I love You, Lord, and I thank You. Amen.

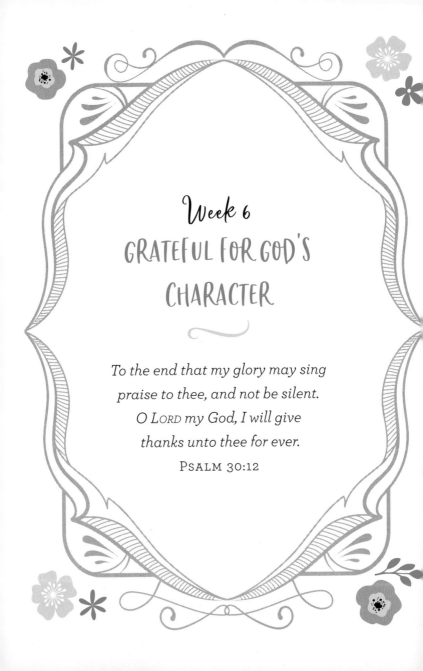

Week 6
GRATEFUL FOR GOD'S CHARACTER

*To the end that my glory may sing
praise to thee, and not be silent.
O LORD my God, I will give
thanks unto thee for ever.*

PSALM 30:12

Week 6: DAY ONE
HOW GREAT IS OUR GOD?

Chris Tomlin got the idea for his award-winning worship song "How Great Is Our God" while meditating on Psalm 104, a praise song written by King David. These two song writers, thousands of years apart, did their best to put into words the glory and power of God.

Tomlin begins his song with a description of God clothed in majesty and wrapped in light. David's words in Psalm 104 present a similar image. He writes: "Praise the Lord, O my soul! O Lord my God, You are very great. You are dressed with great honor and wonderful power. [God] covers Himself with light as with a coat. He spreads out the heavens like a tent. He makes His home on the waters. He makes the clouds His wagon. He rides on the wings of the wind. He makes the winds carry His news" (Psalm 104:1–4 NLV). David goes on describing God's power over the earth, seas, mountains, valleys, and rivers. He says God provides food and water to sustain life. God makes available safe places for animals to dwell and build their nests. He meets the needs of all the earth's creatures as well as mankind. God makes the seasons. He controls the sun and moon, night and day. "O Lord," David exclaims, "how many are Your works! You made them all in wisdom. The earth is full of what You have made" (Psalm 104:24 NLV). Tomlin's song isn't as grandiose as David's, but his message is the same—how great is our God!

David's psalm and Chris Tomlin's song both try to convey God's excellence, but as beautiful as the words are, they fall short. There are no words to adequately describe God's greatness. We can't begin to understand all that He is and everything He does.

God is enormous beyond our imagination, vast, infinite. He is all-powerful, all-knowing, ever-present, and endlessly perfect. The beauty of God's creation pales when compared to the beauty of God Himself.

David ends Psalm 104 with "I will sing to the Lord all my life. I will sing praise to my God as long as I live. May the words of my heart be pleasing to Him. . . . Honor the Lord, O my soul! Praise the Lord!" (Psalm 104:33–35 NLV).

It is appropriate that we devote this final week of *Writing Gratitude on My Heart* to studying the greatness of God, specifically the character traits that make Him the Great I AM (Exodus 3:14). This week as we examine God's power and His presence in our lives, we'll explore the best reasons to be grateful to Him, reasons that lead us to pray, in more contemporary words, this week's memory verse: "I thank you from my heart, and I will never stop singing your praises, my LORD and my God" (Psalm 30:12 CEV).

To the end that my glory may sing praise to thee, and not be silent. O LORD my God, I will give thanks unto thee for ever.
PSALM 30:12

❧ The Blank Page ❧

You've spent the past five weeks reading and learning about gratefulness. You did some self-reflection, and maybe you found a few areas where your gratefulness can improve. The activities you completed helped you to apply gratefulness to your daily life.

Today, spend time thinking about what you learned. Here are some questions to guide you.

* *What does it mean to have a grateful heart?*

* *How has practicing gratefulness improved your relationships?*

* *Einstein said, "There are two ways to live: as though nothing is a miracle, or as though everything is a miracle." Do you view life as if everything is a miracle?*

* *Comparing your current life season to the previous one, how has your gratefulness changed?*

* *How will gratitude help you build godly character traits?*

Make notes about the ideas you've gathered from each week. Then answer two more questions:

* *Am I more grateful today than I was five weeks ago?*

* *In which areas of my life do I need to become more grateful?*

The Last Word

Have you written on your heart all six of the weekly memory verses? Here they are again. Review them and, if necessary, continue to work at memorizing them.

Week One: "Thou art my God, and I will praise thee: thou art my God, I will exalt thee" (Psalm 118:28).

Week Two: "We give thanks to God always for you all, making mention of you in our prayers" (1 Thessalonians 1:2).

Week Three: "I would seek unto God, and unto God would I commit my cause: which doeth great things and unsearchable; marvellous things without number" (Job 5:8–9).

Week Four: "Unto thee, O God, do we give thanks, unto thee do we give thanks: for that thy name is near thy wondrous works declare" (Psalm 75:1).

Week Five: "O come, let us worship and bow down: let us kneel before the LORD our maker. For he is our God; and we are the people of his pasture, and the sheep of his hand" (Psalm 95:6–7).

This Week: "To the end that my glory may sing praise to thee, and not be silent. O LORD my God, I will give thanks unto thee for ever" (Psalm 30:12).

Week 6: DAY TWO
OUR GREAT AND POWERFUL GOD

If you've seen the classic movie *The Wizard of Oz*, you'll remember the moment Dorothy and her friends finally meet the Wizard. A deep and frightening voice thunders from behind a curtain of smoke and flames, "I am Oz, the great and powerful—who are *you*?" Dorothy answers, "I am Dorothy, the small and meek." Then the wizard commands the Tin Man to step forward. "You dare to come to me for a heart, you clinking, clanking, clattering collection of caliginous junk!"[32] His harsh words cause the Tin Man to shiver with fear. A few people might view this scene and compare it with their image of God: He's nothing more than an angry, frightening voice that belittles anyone who dares to ask for His favor. But that's not who God is.

Does God get angry? Yes, and He has the power to frighten and even destroy; however, that's not His plan. The enemy, Satan, is the evil one who wants power over us. He is the one who makes us afraid, wanting us to imagine God as angry, shouting at us, belittling us for not being good enough. Nothing could be further from who God is! He is good and loving toward us. God uses His power against evil. The same God who parted the Red Sea and saved the Israelites from slavery is working on our behalf today. He wants to use His power to help us, not to harm us (Jeremiah 29:11). Instead of being afraid of God's power, there are many reasons to be grateful for it.

---

32 "Meeting the Wizard of Oz," January 28, 2019, YouTube video, 0:15, https://youtu.be/I-WX5-WexvE.

If we have faith that God can do anything, then we know that nothing is impossible. When we feel weak, God gives us power to help us be strong. He gives us strength to reach and even exceed our goals, forgive the unforgivable, move forward in courage, resist temptation, and stand unwavering in adversity. The possibilities of His power are limitless. His power is evident all around us. He causes earth and the heavens to stay in place; He controls sunrises, sunsets, weather, energy; He keeps our bodies alive and working; He provides animals their instincts to live in the wild. There is nothing greater and more powerful than God! Not only does He have power over everything, but He exercises His power flawlessly. His power works through us to make His world a better place. If we are obedient to God and willing to serve Him, He will empower us to do good work for His glory.

To connect with God's power, it's necessary that you come to Him like Dorothy did, small and meek. Unlike the scary Wizard in Oz, God will extend His hand toward you and ask you to step forward in faith. When you give Him power over your life, He can do far more than you dare to ask or imagine.

Thank God for His power working in and around you. Give thanks to the great and all-powerful God!

To the end that my glory may sing praise to thee, and not be silent. O LORD my God, I will give thanks unto thee for ever.
PSALM 30:12

The Blank Page

"O Lord, You have great power, shining-greatness and strength. Yes, everything in heaven and on earth belongs to You. You are the King, O Lord. And You are honored as head over all" (1 Chronicles 29:11 NLV).

Answering the following questions will help you identify specific ways God's mighty power is at work in your life.

* *God uses His power to answer prayers. Considering the seasons of your life, can you list two or three prayer requests that God has answered?*

* *God uses His power to heal. Can you think of a time He healed you either physically, emotionally, or spiritually?*

* *God uses His power to bring about change. What positive changes has God brought into your life?*

* *God uses His power to strengthen you. In what ways has He made you stronger?*

* *God's power is ever present in nature. Look outside. Can you identify three signs of His power?*

* *Jesus is proof that God uses His power to resurrect. Has God resurrected within you an old idea, interest, or desire that you thought was dead?*

* *God uses His power to work through you. Has He given you power to use your skills, wisdom, and talent to enhance the lives of others?*

* *God's power is all around you! Have you found some additional reasons to be grateful?*

The Last Word

Here are ten ways to experience more of God's power in your life:

1. Study God's powerful works in the Bible: He parted the sea (Exodus 14), made the sun stand still (Joshua 10), rescued Daniel from the lions' den (Daniel 6), and allowed Peter to walk on water (Matthew 14). As you read your Bible, you will find many more examples. Keep in mind that this same God is your source of power.

2. Believe in God's goodness.

3. Surrender yourself to His power.

4. Pray for strength and guidance.

5. Step out in faith.

6. Be grateful for your blessings.

7. Reflect on times you recognized God's power at work in your life.

8. Shut out any negative thoughts.

9. Let go of the past.

10. Serve others.

Week 6: DAY THREE
OUR EVER-PRESENT AND ALL-KNOWING GOD

Everywhere. All the time. That is our God. Our loving heavenly Father is constantly with us, not only seeing us but always knowing our thoughts and working in our best interests. What a powerful reason to be grateful!

"What is the very root of this religion? It is Immanuel, God with us! God in man! Heaven connected with earth! The unspeakable union of mortal with immortal." Those are the words of the great evangelist John Wesley. It took many years for Wesley to really know God. He had knowledge of Him from studying the Bible. He preached about God. But something was missing. Wesley searched his soul looking for answers until he finally understood that he didn't have to earn God's love. It was there, always available to him unconditionally. God knew Wesley's every thought and action, and still—God stayed! Wesley knew he didn't deserve God's presence and favor, but it was there. God would always be with him, and Jesus made it possible for Wesley to be with God forever. With his heart opened to God's unconditional, all-knowing, and ever-present love, Wesley preached that message for the next fifty years. Even on his deathbed, at age eighty-eight, Wesley said, "The best thing of all is God is with us."

That *is* the best thing of all—and the best reason of all to thank God. He promises to be with us. He says, "Do not fear, for I am with you. Do not be afraid, for I am your God. I will give you strength, and for sure I will help you" (Isaiah 41:10 NLV). What a comforting thought, knowing that God is always with us, telling us not to be afraid, and promising His help.

Maybe at some time in your life you've thought, like John Wesley, that if you didn't please God, He might abandon you. From the beginning, when God created Adam and Eve, He has never abandoned His creation or His people. He ultimately sent Jesus so, instead of just being with us, God's Holy Spirit could live in our hearts in a personal and intimate way.

If you have accepted Jesus as your Lord and Savior, then you already have God in your heart. You will be one with Him forever, your spirit connected with His. If you haven't accepted Jesus, God still knows you and your thoughts. He is aware and present all the time. Nothing happens on earth without His knowing (Matthew 10:29). If, like Wesley, you sense something missing, maybe it is that intimate relationship with God, recognizing that His love for you is unconditional and you don't have to earn it. Jesus is all you need to take the step from God-all-around-you to God living in you.

God is with you all the time and God is good all the time. Give thanks to Him for His presence. Be grateful that He wants to live in your heart.

To the end that my glory may sing praise to thee, and not be silent. O Lord my God, I will give thanks unto thee for ever.
Psalm 30:12

The Blank Page

Carry with you a small, significant object to remind you of God's presence. Here are some ideas.

- *A pocket-sized New Testament to assure Jesus' words are accessible to you at all times.*

- *A stone symbolizing that you are safe in God's presence. "My safe place is in God, the rock of my strength" (Psalm 62:7 NLV).*

- *A cross to remind you of Jesus' words just before He ascended into heaven: "And I am with you always, even to the end of the world" (Matthew 28:20 NLV).*

- *A small card on which you have written John Wesley's words: "The best thing of all is God is with us."*

- *A ring or other circular object to remind you that God's presence and His love for you are never-ending.*

- *A heart to remind you that God lives inside your heart. He is always with you.*

Use these and other symbols to remind yourself of God's presence, but don't allow the false notion that they in some way will protect you or bring about good. Put your confidence in God alone. Remember His words in Hebrews 13:5 (NIV): "Never will I leave you; never will I forsake you."

❧ The Last Word ❧

"Where can I go from your Spirit? Where can I flee from your presence? If I go up to the heavens, you are there; if I make my bed in the depths, you are there. If I rise on the wings of the dawn, if I settle on the far side of the sea, even there your hand will guide me, your right hand will hold me fast. If I say, 'Surely the darkness will hide me and the light become night around me,' even the darkness will not be dark to you; the night will shine like the day, for darkness is as light to you" (Psalm 139:7–12 NIV).

David's message in Psalm 139 is simple: You can't run from God. He is everywhere. That's a good thing if you remember, as John Wesley did, that God will love and forgive you in spite of your sins. God sees everything you do, and you don't have to run from Him. You couldn't get away from Him even if you tried.

Embrace the comforting thought that whether you are in a plane flying above the earth or if you're diving the Great Barrier Reef, God is there. Wherever you travel, He is your travel guide. If you decide to stay home, God is there too. Be grateful that He is with you right now, wherever you are.

Week 6: DAY FOUR
OUR INFINITELY FAITHFUL GOD

Do you recognize the name Thomas Chisholm? If not, you likely recognize the title of his hymn "Great Is Thy Faithfulness." Chisholm, an ordained minister, wrote more than 1,200 poems, among them "Great Is Thy Faithfulness." When Reverend William H. Runyan, at the Moody Bible Institute in Chicago, read "Great Is Thy Faithfulness," it was so pleasing to him that he set it to music. George Beverly Shea, the famous singer with Billy Graham's crusades, introduced the song at a meeting in Great Britain, and from there its popularity grew. Years later, Runyan wrote, "This particular poem held such an appeal that I prayed most earnestly that my tune might carry over its message in a worthy way, and the subsequent history of its use indicates that God answered [my] prayer." God in His faithfulness had used Chisholm's, Runyan's, and Shea's combined talents to spread His message to the world: "I Am your faithful God."

> *Great is thy faithfulness! Great is thy faithfulness!*
> *Morning by morning new mercies I see;*
> *All I have needed thy hand hath provided;*
> *Great is thy faithfulness, Lord, unto me![33]*

The words come from Lamentations 3:22–23 (NLV): "It is because of the Lord's loving-kindness that we are not destroyed for His loving-pity never ends. It is new every morning. He is so very faithful."

---

33 C. Michael Hawn, "History of Hymns: 'Great Is Thy Faithfulness,'" August 23, 2013, https://www.umcdiscipleship.org/resources/history-of-hymns-great-is-thy-faithfulness.

God is always faithful—another reason for gratitude! His "loving-pity" (His mercy) never ends. He is infinitely wise. You can trust Him to provide what is right for you in all circumstances. He is present with you, watching over you and listening when you pray. There's no need too small or too trivial that it isn't important to Him. God so faithfully pours blessings into your life, and His faithfulness carries you through the rough times.

Faithfulness isn't what God does. It's who He is! Exodus 16 tells about the Israelites needing food as they traveled to the Promised Land. They grumbled, wishing they had never left Egypt, where there were pots of meat and all the food they wanted. God saw how weak their faith was. Still, He provided for their needs. A huge flock of quail landed in their camp. They had meat. Then bread rained from heaven. It was a very big deal because it literally saved the whole tribe of Israelites from starving to death. They praised God joyfully for a while, but as the Israelites' story continues in the Bible, we discover numerous times when their faith in God waned. Still, God remained faithful to them and still remains faithful to all of us!

Think about God's faithfulness to you. What has He saved you from? What blessings has He brought into your life? Give thanks to Him for His unending faithfulness. Thank God for His infinite wisdom, guidance, and care.

To the end that my glory may sing praise to thee, and not be silent. O LORD my God, I will give thanks unto thee for ever.
PSALM 30:12

The Blank Page

It took many years for "Great Is Thy Faithfulness" to become a success. It was first published in 1928, but it was 1954 before Shea's singing made it popular all over the world. Needless to say, Thomas Chisholm did not make a lot of money from the song. He died in 1960. Nearing the end of his life, he wrote, "My income has not been large at any time due to impaired health in the earlier years which has followed me on until now. Although I must not fail to record here the unfailing faithfulness of a covenant-keeping God and that He has given me many wonderful displays of His providing care, for which I am filled with astonishing gratefulness."[34]

Today's challenge is to think about the past seven days and list times when God was faithful to meet your specific needs. Think about times when God met your need without intervention from others. For example, a time when you found something you thought you lost or an ingredient for cooking you thought you didn't have. Think about times when God met your needs through someone else. Maybe you dreaded having to interrupt your work to drive your kids to an activity and a friend called suggesting she drive your kids along with hers.

God is faithful every day. Whenever you recognize His faithfulness, thank Him. Noticing the ways in which He is faithful to you helps build your faith in Him.

---

34 Kenneth W. Osbeck, *101 Hymn Stories* (Grand Rapids, MI: Kregel Publications, 1982), 84.

❧ The Last Word ❧

You've used all six memory cards and applied the memory tips offered in *Writing Gratitude on My Heart*, but your commitment to memorizing scripture is just beginning. Keep at it. Promise yourself and God you will continue to memorize at least one verse each week.

The Bible speaks about itself in scripture.

- ✳ *"Thy word is true from the beginning"* (Psalm 119:160).
- ✳ *"Every word of God is pure"* (Proverbs 30:5).
- ✳ *"For the word of God is quick, and powerful, and sharper than any twoedged sword"* (Hebrews 4:12).
- ✳ *"The entrance of thy words giveth light; it giveth understanding unto the simple"* (Psalm 119:130).
- ✳ *"Heaven and earth shall pass away, but my words shall not pass away"* (Matthew 24:35).

In the New Testament, James says, "Obey God's message! Don't fool yourselves by just listening to it" (James 1:22 CEV). Put your memory verses into action. Knowing what's in the Bible and using it every day is the key reason to memorize scripture. You can't apply what God tells you unless you remember His instructions. His instructions are always perfect and good. You can trust them to faithfully guide you through every step of life.

Here is one more verse for you to remember: "Know therefore that the LORD your God is God; he is the faithful God, keeping his covenant of love to a thousand generations of those who love him and keep his commandments" (Deuteronomy 7:9 NIV).

Week 6: DAY FIVE
OUR PERFECT GOD

Perfect. Webster's dictionary defines it as "being entirely without fault or defect." There is no one on earth who fits that definition. When Adam and Eve ate fruit from the Tree of Knowledge of Good and Evil, earthly perfection became impossible. Sin entered the world, and sin and perfection cannot coexist.

God remains the only One who is infinitely perfect. Everything He is and does is perfect (Psalm 18:30). His character is perfect. He is always perfectly fair, determined, compassionate, strong, faithful, and forgiving. He is perfect in power, presence, wisdom, and love.

The ancient generations did their best to please God by trying to measure up to His sinless, blameless model of perfection, but of course they failed. Nobody's perfect. Because God loves us, He sent Jesus, who willingly took the blame for our sin and made us perfect in God's sight. Because of Jesus' sacrifice and with Him as our Savior, we are as perfect as we can be here on earth. We exist by the mercy of God's love, and we won't achieve a sinless level of perfection until we get to heaven.

Still, in Matthew 5:48 (NLV), Jesus says, "You must be perfect as your Father in heaven is perfect." What does that mean? It means to do your best to imitate God's loving character. Love is the essence of who God is (1 John 4:8). You can strive toward perfection by practicing love. Jesus told His followers the greatest commandment of all is "Love the Lord your God with all your heart" and "You must love your neighbor as you love yourself" (Matthew 22:37–39 NLV).

In love and everything else, you can't come near God's standard of perfection; the best you can do is try. C. S. Lewis said God knows we aren't perfect. Every time we fall if we ask God to pick us up again He will. On the other hand, Lewis said, we need to understand that God leads us toward absolute perfection. We are the ones who prevent God from taking us to that goal.[35]

God doesn't expect you to be perfectly perfect. By His grace you can accept your imperfections knowing you will be made perfect in heaven. In the meantime, you can be grateful for Jesus, who makes you perfect in God's sight, and you can be grateful to God that He loves you right now, just the way you are.

"Thank You, dear God, for loving me regardless of my imperfection. Thank You for always being faithful and perfect in every way. Please help me to become more like You. Amen."

To the end that my glory may sing praise to thee, and not be silent. O LORD my God, I will give thanks unto thee for ever.

PSALM 30:12

35   C. S. Lewis, *Mere Christianity* (New York: HarperCollins, 2001), retrieved from https://f1lt3r. github.io/mere-christianity/book-4/MereChristianity-Book4-Chapters9-10.pdf.

❧ The Blank Page ❧

In *My Utmost for His Highest*, Oswald Chambers wrote: "It is a trap to presume that God wants to make us perfect specimens of what He can do—God's purpose is to make us one with Himself.... Christian perfection is not, and never can be, human perfection. Christian perfection is the perfection of a relationship with God that shows itself to be true even amid the seemingly unimportant aspects of human life."[36]

Thinking about Chambers's words and today's devotion, answer these questions:

* *How do you define perfection?*
* *Is there an area in your life where you are trying to be perfect?*
* *Are you at peace with the idea that you are imperfect?*
* *Does God want you to be perfect?*
* *Will you ever be perfect? Why or why not?*
* *Do you see God working within you and changing you for the better?*
* *Do you believe God is leading you to work on your character to become more like Him?*
* *Which is the most important of God's characteristics to emulate?*
* *What can you do to have a more perfect relationship with God?*
* *Do you believe that God is perfect in every way?*
* *How can you show gratitude to God for the perfect way He loves and provides for you?*

---

36   Oswald Chambers, "Christian Perfection," My Utmost for His Highest, https://utmost.org/christian-perfection/.

❧ The Last Word ❧

This week's memory verse says, "To the end that my glory may sing praise to thee, and not be silent. O LORD my God, I will give thanks unto thee for ever" (Psalm 30:12). Gratefulness is not meant to be silent. It should be offered to God and shared with others. Bring the idea of thankfulness into your conversations. Tell your family and friends what you've learned about gratefulness. Share with them some of the reasons you are grateful.

Read what others have said about expressing gratitude.

* *"Feeling gratitude and not expressing it is like wrapping a present and not giving it."* [37] *—William Arthur Ward*

* *"We must find time to stop and thank the people who make a difference in our lives."* [38] *—John F. Kennedy*

* *"Appreciation can make a day, even change a life. Your willingness to put it into words is all that is necessary."* [39] *—Margaret Cousins*

* *"The more you recognize and express gratitude for the things you have, the more things you will have to express gratitude for."* [40] *—Zig Ziglar*

* *"Train yourself never to put off the word or action for the expression of gratitude."* [41] *—Albert Schweitzer*

* *"Showing gratitude is one of the simplest yet most powerful things humans can do for each other."* [42] *—Randy Pausch*

37   William Arthur Ward, Brainy Quote, https://www.brainyquote.com/quotes/william_arthur_ward_105516.

38   Kennedy Center Facebook page, https://www.facebook.com/KennedyCenter/posts/we-must-find-time-to-stop-and-thank-the-people-who-make-a-difference-in-our-live/10157462999460865/.

39   Nina Lesowitz & Mary Beth Sammons, *The Grateful Life* (Jersey City, NJ: Viva Editions, 2014).

40   Zig Ziglar, *Over the Top: Moving from Survival to Stability, from Stability to Success, from Success to Significance*, rev. ed. (Nashville, TN: Thomas Nelson, 2007), 150.

41   Albert Schweitzer, Inspiring Quotes, https://www.inspiringquotes.us/author/3148-albert-schweitzer/about-gratitude.

42   Randy Pausch, AZ Quotes, https://www.azquotes.com/quote/362819.

Week 6: DAY Six
OUR BEAUTIFUL GOD

Several years ago, *Forbes* did an article called "21 Most Beautiful Places in the World to Visit." Included among others were destinations like Longsheng, China, where terraced rice fields resemble dragon scales; the Amazon River and its surrounding rain forests; Iceland, for the Northern Lights; and closer to home, Yellowstone National Park in Wyoming. In addition to natural wonders, the article cites beautiful architectural works: temples, castles, pyramids. Wherever you go in the world, wherever you are right now, there is something beautiful.

There's an old phrase, beauty is in the eye of the beholder. We all perceive beauty differently. For some, beauty is found in nature. For others, beauty is art—paintings, photographs, sculptures—or music or theater. Beauty can be found in words woven together to make poetry and novels. It can be in the intricacies of how things work or in how things taste or smell. Some people find new buildings beautiful, and others are drawn to the beauty of ancient ruins. Whether you find beauty in any of these things or in relationships, feelings, or ideas, you will agree that beauty is everywhere.

All beauty is a reflection of God. While we don't know what God looks like, we know that everything about Him is beautiful. The Bible says God shines from heaven, perfect in beauty (Psalm 50:2). "He is as bright as the sun. He has light shining from His hand, where His power is hidden" (Habakkuk 3:4 NLV).

You've been studying God's character this week. All of His attributes, His traits, are beautiful. His love for His earth and mankind is beautiful. The nearer we get to God and as we try to imitate His characteristics, the more beauty we see. Saint Thomas Aquinas explains it this way: "If a person, upon entering a certain house, should feel a warmth at the door of the house, and going within should feel a greater warmth, and so on the more he went into its interior, he would believe that somewhere within was a fire, even if he did not see the fire itself which caused this heat which he felt. So also is it when we consider the things of this world. For one finds all things arranged in different degrees of beauty and worth, and the closer things approach to God, the more beautiful and better they are found to be. Thus, the heavenly bodies are more beautiful and nobler than those which are below them; and, likewise, the invisible things in relation to the visible. Therefore, it must be seen that all these things proceed from one God who gives His being and beauty to each and everything."[43]

You can't see God, but He is everywhere in His beautiful works! Give thanks to Him, and savor the beauty He sets around you. One day in heaven you will see God with your own eyes and know just how beautiful He really is (Psalm 27:4).

To the end that my glory may sing praise to thee, and not be silent. O LORD my God, I will give thanks unto thee for ever.
PSALM 30:12

43   Thomas Aquinas, "St. Thomas Aquinas on the Apostle's Creed," Patristic Bible Commentary, https://sites.google.com/site/aquinasstudybible/apostle-s-creed/st-thomas-aquinas-on-the-apostle-s-creed.

❧ The Blank Page ❧

Your assignment today is to do something to add more beauty to the world. Here are twenty ideas to choose from. See if you can come up with more.

1. Plant something.
2. Forgive someone.
3. Create a work of art.
4. Sing, or play a musical instrument.
5. Photograph some beautiful places near your home and share them on social media.
6. Lead someone to Christ.
7. Help someone in need.
8. Smile!
9. Love others, especially those with whom you have differences.
10. Plan a special surprise for someone.
11. Laugh more.
12. Clean up a mess!
13. Don't allow anger to take root in your heart.
14. Listen with caring and compassion.
15. Have spontaneous fun with your spouse and your kids.
16. Don't take yourself too seriously.
17. Help others find reasons to be grateful.
18. Make something shabby look like new.
19. Pray for others.
20. Make a new friend.

"Worship the Lord in the beauty of holy living" (Psalm 29:2 NLV).

The Last Word

"All Things Bright and Beautiful"

BY CECIL FRANCES ALEXANDER (1848)

All things bright and beautiful,
all creatures great and small,
all things wise and wonderful,
the Lord God made them all.
Each little flower that opens,
each little bird that sings,
he made their glowing colors,
he made their tiny wings.
The purple-headed mountain,
the river running by,
the sunset, and the morning
that brightens up the sky.
The cold wind in the winter,
the pleasant summer sun,
the ripe fruits in the garden,
he made them, every one.
The tall trees in the greenwood,
the meadows where we play,
the flowers by the water
we gather every day.
He gave us eyes to see them,
and lips that we might tell
how great is God Almighty,
who has made all things well.

Week 6: DAY SEVEN
PUTTING IT ALL TOGETHER

You have come to the end of this six-week Bible memory devotional. Along with the verses on your scripture memory cards, you've read and thought about many other Bible verses. Keep adding to your bank of memorized scripture.

Working through *Writing Gratitude on My Heart*, you've given much thought to gratitude, what it means and how to live a truly grateful life. You contemplated the ideas that true gratefulness is thanking God for life, finding joy in living, and practicing gratitude even when life becomes stressful. You brought more gratitude into your relationships with your children, spouse, friends, people in your community, and strangers. How you define miracles might have changed as you've thought about gratitude and discovered new things to be grateful for.

You learned that God's love is at the heart of all gratefulness, and a grateful heart comes from knowing Him, loving Him, and working at becoming more like Him. *Writing Gratitude on My Heart* has led you deeper into your relationship with God. In these past several weeks, you've put even more effort into connecting with Him, and hopefully, you will continue to do so. Your relationship with God affects every aspect of your life.

You have thought about the seasons of life and how gratefulness shapes them. You've done a lot of soul searching and discovered that you are God's beautiful work-in-progress, a work that never ends. As you've explored your character traits, you might have committed to making a few changes. Maybe you discovered that your degree of gratefulness needed to be bumped up a little. When you become more grateful, it leads to a transformed life, one more aligned with God and all His positive attributes.

During this last week, you've explored the greatness of God, specifically the character traits that make Him the Great I Am. God is responsible for every good thing! He is the only One worthy of your grateful praise and exaltation. He alone is pure, perfect, and good. God is merciful toward you and forgiving. His love for you is forever! Everything you have is a blessing from Him. All of your good traits, your talents, and your skills are His gifts to you. Each day, you find new reasons to be grateful to Him as you grow more aware of all the good ways He is at work in and around you. How great is your God! When you express your gratitude to Him, your love for Him grows.

"To the end that my glory may sing praise to thee, and not be silent. O LORD my God, I will give thanks unto thee for ever" (Psalm 30:12). Can you hear the psalmist David speaking to you in this verse? He is telling you, "Until you take your last breath, give thanks to God!" In everything, give thanks to Him. Write gratitude on your heart. Remember not to allow one blessing, one miracle, or one recognition of God's presence in your life to pass without thanks.

To the end that my glory may sing praise to thee, and not be silent. O LORD my God, I will give thanks unto thee for ever.
PSALM 30:12

The Blank Page

Here are ten final questions to think about:

1. How do you define gratefulness?

2. Why is God the essence of gratefulness?

3. Can you name several miracles in your life you are grateful for?

4. How can gratefulness improve your relationships?

5. How can gratefulness help you get through hard times?

6. How can you show more gratefulness to God?

7. Why is scripture memorization important?

8. What is your best technique for memorizing scripture?

9. What are three different ways to share scripture with others?

10. What is the most important thing you've learned from this six-week devotional study?

The Last Word

"Thanks to God"

BY AUGUST L. STORM

(former lieutenant colonel in the Salvation Army)

Thanks to God for my Redeemer,
Thanks for all Thou dost provide!
Thanks for times now but a memory,
Thanks for Jesus by my side!
Thanks for pleasant, balmy springtime,
Thanks for dark and stormy fall!
Thanks for tears by now forgotten,
Thanks for peace within my soul!
Thanks for prayers that Thou hast answered,
Thanks for what Thou dost deny!
Thanks for storms that I have weathered,
Thanks for all Thou dost supply!
Thanks for pain, and thanks for pleasure,
Thanks for comfort in despair!
Thanks for grace that none can measure,
Thanks for love beyond compare!
Thanks for roses by the wayside,
Thanks for thorns their stems contain!
Thanks for home and thanks for fireside,
Thanks for hope, that sweet refrain!
Thanks for joy and thanks for sorrow,
Thanks for heavenly peace with Thee!
Thanks for hope in the tomorrow,
Thanks through all eternity![44]

"I thank You from my heart, and I will never stop singing
Your praises, my Lord and my God. Amen."

---

44   William and Ardythe Petersen, *The Complete Book of Hymns* (Carol Stream, IL: Tyndale House, 2006), 662.

Thou art my God, and I will praise thee:
Thou art my God, I will exalt thee.

Psalm 118:28

WE GIVE THANKS TO GOD ALWAYS FOR YOU ALL, MAKING MENTION OF YOU IN OUR PRAYERS.

1 THESSALONIANS 1:2